MW01292977

STAGGERING

Life and Death on the Texas Frontier at Staggers Point

BY AVREL SEALE

For my loving father, Bradford Carl Seale,
who passed this blood to me,

and for my loving mother, Jan Seale,
who passed the ink ...

Copyright 2014

ISBN 978-1-312-74442-4

Contents

Acknowledgements

THE HISTORY CONTAINED IN THESE PAGES has only survived to be compiled by me because of the loving stewardship of many dozens of descendants, most of whom, of course, are now passed away. In the top tier of those stewards of this history were newspaper columnist Jimmie Henry Rice, Sam Rice, Robert Henry Seale, Ola Maye Henry, and Effie Rice Rambo, all of whom passed into that horse and cattle ranch in the great beyond before this subject had attracted my attention.

Happily, though, many latter-day historians are still with us as of this writing. I would like to acknowledge the extensive research into the Seale family done by Jim Boyd, who published his findings in his 2004 book *Grandfather's Journal: The Record of the First Seales in Texas*. I also wish to acknowledge Randi Smith and her contemporaries for their preservation of Henry family history, especially with the 1992 publication of *American Descendants of James and Margot (O'Hara) Henry of County Antrim, Ireland*.

I also thank the following for their help, encouragement, and contributions of material: Anne Seale Burkhart and Edsel Burkhart (deceased), who unknowingly planted the seed of this book in me thirty years ago, their daughter Anne Yoder, Betty Westbrook Trant, Mervin Peters, Kathryn Seale, Nan Ross of the Carnegie History Center of Bryan, Don Carleton, director of the Briscoe Center for American History at The University of Texas at Austin; the reference librarians of the Briscoe Center for American History and University of Texas Libraries; and Retha Valero of Top of the Hill Grocery and Cafe, who makes the best hamburger in

Benchley, Texas.

Most of all, my thanks and love go to my wife, Kirstin, for her support and encouragement in allowing me those many trips to Bryan, and to my three sons — Andrew, Cameron, and Ian — for gamely traipsing behind Dad through many an overgrown cemetery. These are your people.

The signature of Robert Henry,
on a legal document from 1837

The signature of Eli Seale,
on a petition to the Texas Congress in 1840

STAGGERING

1.

Visitors

*"Ah, those old memories, how they throng
around me, bringing up forms and faces long
since hidden 'neath the sod."*

—*Noah Smithwick*
The Evolution of a State, *1900*[1]

JUST BEFORE DARK, a large band of Comanches gathered at the entrance to the plantation. Their number must have been significant because Bettie, working in and around her log cabin, saw them at nearly a mile away. Here in east-central Texas, at the "bleeding edge" of the frontier, this sight was never good news.

Sometimes, elsewhere in the surrounding country, Indians of various tribes swooped down on horseback by the

---

[1] Eugene Barker, ed. *Texas History*, (Dallas: The Southwest Press, 1929) p. 146.

light of a full moon, screaming as they laid waste to settlements, screaming like the banshees the Irish had always spoken of but probably didn't believe in until now. At other times they came like this, in daylight, by the front door, occasionally even holding a white flag or offering an introductory handshake, before torturing the men to death, raping the women, kidnapping the children, stealing the horses, and burning the settlement to the ground. The most famous such raid in history, on the Parker family's fort, had taken place probably only a year earlier and less than sixty miles to the north.[2]

Even closer, in Bettie's own area that would become Robertson County, and possibly this same year, an Indian party had approached the Harvey family's home, also at suppertime. Mr. Harvey ran for his gun resting above the doorway but was hit in the neck with a bullet and killed instantly. His wife hid under the bed, but the Indians dragged her out, killed and scalped her, then cut out her heart and laid it on her breast. Their ten-year-old boy was found with more than twenty bullet holes in his jacket. And their daughter was carried off to live for more than a year with the Indians before being sold to Mexicans. (Through an epic effort, her uncle eventually recovered her, and she returned to live near the scene of the crime.)[3]

Bettie knew at once what had attracted the visitors and immediately sent one of her children to tell the men working near the pasture to hide the horses in the brush.[4] The Henrys were horse people, going back to the childhood of Bettie's husband, Robert, in northern Ireland. And here at Staggers Point — the Irish settlement along the Little

---

[2] S.G. Gwynn, *Empire of the Summer Moon*, 2010.

[3] J.W. Wilbarger, *Indian Depredations in Texas*, (Austin: Hutchings Printing House, 1889), p. 230. There are numerous iterations of this story, largely thought to be the basis for the movie *The Searchers*. These stories vary in their details.

[4] In another version, she sends two of her sons to lead the horses into the woods to hide them, instructing them not to come out nor allow the horses to graze until word came from her." Betty Westbrook Trant Family Papers, p. 1.

Brazos River[5] near modern Bryan, Texas — horses abounded, good ones. In this wilderness in the Mexican state of "Coahuila y Tejas" — or as the settlers wrote it, "Cowheela, Texas" — they would soon even have a racetrack.

To the Indians who made hunting and raiding forays into this area — Comanche, Kiowa, Lipan Apache, Waco, Anadarko — horses were the ultimate currency, both wealth and military might in a single package, one that not only moved under its own power, but moved them, and that they could steal with relative ease and drive in giant herds known as *remudas* over hundreds of miles back to their home grounds. Horse-rich and human-poor, Staggers Point in the 1830s and 1840s was an irresistible target. And of all the Indians, these Comanches were the most feared, and for reason. [6] [7]

The child sent to the pasture botched the message and failed to convey the presence of Indians at all. Sensing no danger, the men turned the horses loose so that they might trot up to the house, a sight that normally would have pleased Bettie.

The Comanche band was on the farm now and had closed to within a half mile. Realizing the mistake, Bettie ran to the lot, turned all the horses inside the corral, and drove them into the big stable, which had a one-pound lock with a key some eight inches long.

The Comanches had surrounded the cabin now. She heard their steps behind her but went on, urging the horses to pass into the barn, pushing and slapping their haunches. As she pushed the last one in, adrenaline coursing through

---

[5] The Little Brazos River is not to be confused with the Brazos River, to which the Little Brazos River empties, or with Little River, also a Brazos tributary upriver.

[6] Myrtle Murray, "Home Life on Early Ranches of Southwest Texas," *The Cattleman* Magazine, February 1940.

[7] Anne Seale Burkhart, "Pioneer Ancestors" (high school paper), May 20, 1939, Bryan, Texas. Compiled from family papers.

her tiny frame, she pushed the door to and locked it. Then, she turned to the one she presumed to be the chief, looked him coolly in the eye, and slipped the key into her pocket.

We don't know what flashed through her mind in that moment, but we can assume she wondered if the Comanches now would rape her, then either kidnap her or perhaps mutilate her alive in ways limited only by their imaginations. This fear would not have been the product of an ugly stereotype but of a well-established precedent, one of which she and all her neighbors would have been only too aware. The best she might have hoped for was a quick and simple end — shot, clubbed, or tomahawked — after which the Indians would go about stealing all of her horses with a workaday nonchalance. Maybe the children would escape through the thickly covered bottomlands along the Little Brazos River and its tributary creeks, and maybe Robert would find them months later holed up in a primitive fort somewhere to the east.

It was frankly crazy for her to be living in this place. To get a sense for just how crazy, we can look to S.C. Gwynne's description of the Parker Fort near modern Groesbeck, which was a little farther north but no farther west than Staggers Point, and whose historic attack occurred *seven years after* the Henrys had settled here on the Little Brazos River:

> The [Parker] fort had another distinction: in the year of Texas independence, it stood on the absolute outermost edge of the Indian frontier. There were no Anglo settlements to the west, no towns, no houses, no permanent structures of any kind save the grass huts of the Wichitas or the makeshift shacks of the Comancheros ... And the fort was so far beyond the ordinary line of settlements that there were hardly any people *behind* it either. ... Whatever small and unresponsive Mexican

forces had once existed were now gone, and the fragile Texas republic had better things to do than protect lunatic Anglo farmers who insisted on living beyond civilization's last outposts.[8]

Bettie would have wondered if this was how it all would end. If all of the risks she and Robert had taken had come to this. If all of the work, the sorrows and the joys had come down to what it had for so many of her kind, a tragic, grisly end.

---

[8] S.C. Gwynne, *Empire of the Summer Moon*, p. 14.

2.

Ireland and Exodus

*"Joy is the will which labors, which overcomes
obstacles, which knows triumph."*

—*William Butler Yeats*

IT HAD BEEN A LONG, IMPROBABLE JOURNEY. Little is known of
her childhood except that Elizabeth Sharon Downing was
born January 30, 1798, probably in northern Ireland's
Londonderry, commonly known as "Derry." (Though many
sources give her birthplace as London, likely the result of
early confusion with "Londonderry," on her gravestone under
"BETTIE HENRY" is etched — in diagonal, sporty type —
"Born in Ireland.") As the daughter of a large-scale linen
miller, she grew up receiving the best education available
there.[9] But we're also told her reading was more extensive
than that of other children due to the direction of her mother,
Elizabeth.[10]

---

[9] Murray, "Home Life on Early Ranches of Southwest Texas"

Robert Henry was born in 1801 in the tiny village of Loughguile near Londonderry to James Henry and Margot O'Hara.[11] It's not clear what brought Robert and Bettie together, but they had at least three things in common: a fierce, muscular Presbyterianism. Their large families were made up of "Bluestocking Presbyterians." During the seventeenth century, when argument raged over whether divine authority rested with the Pope, the king, or the people, the poor "Covenanters" from Scotland wore unbleached woolen stockings in contrast to the richer Episcopalians who wore stockings either dyed black or bleached white. The bluish tint of the untreated wool gave Presbyterians the distinction of "Bluestockings."[12]

Second, they had prominent uncles — she the niece of a Lord Downing who served in the Irish Parliament[13] and he the nephew of Squire O'Hara, who owned a respectable chunk of County Antrim.[14]

Third and perhaps most importantly, they shared a love of horses.[15] Robert had spent a large part of his boyhood caring for his Uncle O'Hara's horses in and around the ancient stone stables of Crebilly Castle.[16]

Whatever brought them together, there was love. On Saturday, June 3, 1820, Bettie and Robert married. Rev. Edward L. Parker (1785-1850) was pastor of a Presbyterian church at the same time and in the same city. He might well

---

[10] Betty Trant Papers, p. 1.

[11] Ola Maye Henry, "The Henry Family," *Brazos County History: Rich Past - Bright Future*, Ed. Glenna Fourman Brundidge, (Bryan: Family History Foundation, 1986) p. 226.

[12] http://en.wikipedia.org/wiki/Talk%3ABluestocking

[13] Burkhart, "Pioneer Ancestors."

[14] Randi Smith, et al., *American Descendants of James and Margot (O'Hara) Henry of County Antrim, Ireland*, (Decorah, Iowa: The Anundsen Publishing Co., 1992) p. iv

[15] Annie Doom Pickrell, *Pioneer Women in Texas* (Austin and New York: Jenkins Publishing Company, The Pemberton Press, 1928, 1970), Chapter "Elizabeth Downing Henry" "Data contributed by Mrs. H.B. Granberry, Austin, Texas."

[16] Smith, *American Ancestors of James and Margot (O'Hara) Henry*, p. 10

have even presided at their nuptials. In his book, *History of Londonderry,* he describes a typical Presbyterian wedding:

> The morning of the marriage day was ushered in with the discharge of musketry, in the respective neighborhoods of the persons who were to be united. This practice it seems originated in Ireland, in consequence of the Catholics having been, after the Revolution, deprived of the use of firearms. The Protestants, proud of the superior privilege which they then enjoyed, made a display of their warlike instruments on all public occasions. Seldom was a respectable man married without his sword by his side.

The groom left home with his wedding party and halfway to her home they were met by her wedding party. The ceremony from there would not have been too foreign to us, until perhaps the climax, when according to Rev. Parker, "Having concluded with another prayer, he requested the groom to salute his bride, which being done, the minister performed the same ceremony, and was immediately followed by the male part of the company; the female in like manner saluted the bridegroom."[17]

Though comically stilted in our mind's eye, this mutual salute, in lieu of a kiss, seems somehow appropriate in prefiguring a life that would require not only military-grade starch but a true and full partnership; indeed, he saluted her first. For every heroic act Robert would perform in the larger political and military dramas of the day, an equally heroic act — or three — would be carried out by Bettie on or near the home front. From the beginning, she would be his equal

---

[17] Edward L. Parker, *History of Londonderry*,
http://www.libraryireland.com/ScotchIrishAmerica/VII-3.php.

in their commitment to a life of unknowns and in the courage and grit that life required. As Mary Austin Holley, Stephen F. Austin's sister, would write just a few years later, "Many a wife in Texas has proved herself the better half, and many a widow's heart has prompted her to daring."[18]

And if there was love, there was also apparently a shared audacity. Sometime before the wedding, they had resolved to come to the New World, first to the United States, and then, as circumstances permitted, farther west to a place they had heard was ripe for farming and ranching and where large parcels of land were free for the asking, Texas. We do not know whether Robert and Bettie stopped to wonder why it came so cheap, and if they had been told, whether they would have proceeded.

It had been the northeasternmost frontier of New Spain but had never been settled, and it seemed as long as it remained Spanish, it never would. The saying of the time was that the Spanish would not permit even a bird to cross the Sabine. But a revolution that had stretched over the previous eleven years had just then made it a part of the new nation of Mexico.

What little was known of Texas up to that point reached Ireland in short excerpts from newspapers in the New World — often from New Orleans, the western edge of the English-speaking world. The region was sometimes referred to in these accounts as "the Texas." One 1816 item in the *Freeman's Journal* quoted Mexican revolutionary Joseph Manuel De Herrera:

> Inhabitants of Texas! be proud that you have been taken under the protection of the Constitution of the Republic. Show yourselves worthy of the rank to which you have been elevated. Fan the sacred flame of Liberty, just kindled in the bosom of our hitherto

---

[18] Mary Austin Holley, *Texas*, p. 146.

unfortunate brethren now emancipated from the chains of despotism. Such conduct will be crowned with the blessings of Heaven.

Obey the laws—comply faithfully and exactly with your contracts—display to the world the honors, humanity, and generosity of your character — cultivate with the utmost care and brotherly intercourse and friendship with the Republic of the North — abstain from all illegal commerce, especially within the United States; every violation of the laws shall be punished with inflexible severity; smugglers and pirates shall suffer death. The friend of liberty, the oppressed, and the brave, shall always find a home and country among the people of Mexico; we will receive with open arms all who respect our laws and independence.

—Josph M. DeHerrera September 18, 1816
Seventh Year of Mexican Independence[19]

Of course, this was quite premature, as Mexico would not be independent for another five years. The 1810s were a baffling time in Texas history, and if your broadsheet newspaper was more than a few months old, you really had no idea who ruled this region. From reports such as the one above, you could be forgiven for thinking that Mexico was already free of Spain and an independent republic, or that it was the "Texas Republic," peopled by United States expatriates. This was the era of Anglo "filibusters" making unauthorized military expeditions into Texas to conquer chunks of it willy-nilly.

French filibusters, too, were antagonizing the Spanish

---

[19] *Freeman's Journal,* December 23, 1816

along the coast and in East Texas. In 1817 the French pirate
Jean Laffite set up his own "republic" on Galveston. His
settlement grew to more than one thousand people but was
abandoned in 1820. In 1818 a band of Napoleonic exiles
under Gen. Charles Lallemand attempted a settlement at
Champ d'Asile, on the Trinity, but it too was abandoned, due
to food shortages and Spanish threats.[20] Someone so disposed
could read any of these reports and believe that Texas would
be something other than Spanish within a few weeks. And
perhaps these Irish families of County Antrim did just that.

As for Texas' aboriginal populations, journals were aware
of their presence, but these populations were nothing to be
concerned about. A November 1819 edition of *Finns Leinster
Journal* in northern Ireland reports, "And even at Barassos
[Brazos?] according to despatches for Colonel Robinson [a
filibuster], the natives had evinced a most friendly
disposition."

SO WHAT MOTIVATED these newlyweds — he twenty, she
twenty-three — to leave their pastoral existence in northern
Ireland for primitive North America? They left no single easy
answer, but several factors probably combined to send them
west. Leaving for the New World was never a decision taken
lightly, and they would have known the transatlantic journey
alone was fraught with danger, and that there was little
chance they would ever again see those they left behind.
Friends, relatives, parents — goodbye was goodbye.

The Henrys' strong identity as Presbyterians and their
roots in the Ulster region that includes all of modern
Northern Ireland marks them as classic "Scots-Irish" or
"Ulster Presbyterians." They are referred to in one source as
"Vester Presbyterians"[21] and in another as "bluestocking

[20] "FRENCH," *Handbook of Texas Online*
(http://www.tshaonline.org/handbook/online/articles/pmf01), accessed June
05, 2014. Uploaded on June 12, 2010. Modified on November 25, 2013.
Published by the Texas State Historical Association

Presbyterians."[22]

The Scots-Irish descended from Scottish and English families who were coaxed by the British to colonize northern Ireland during the "Plantation of Ulster" in the 1600s. Sowing the seeds of violence for centuries to come, it was a classic case of using one troublesome population to suppress a more troublesome one. In this scheme, the Scots, who were second-class citizens, were invited to leave their island and oppress the despised Catholics, third-class citizens, on the neighboring island.

The period of the Henrys' emigration to America — 1821 — falls into a sort of crack of history. Earlier, the 1700s had seen five large waves of emigration of Scots-Irish to America. The descendants of those immigrants would include twelve American presidents, from Andrew Jackson to Richard Nixon. And the Great Potato Famine, which would kill a million Irish and send another million toward Ellis Island, would not begin until 1845. So what would send Ulster Presbyterians to America in the 1820s?

In a history of Brazos County, Texas, Shirlireed Walker writes, "the young families ... left Ireland in 1821 because Irish and English inheritance laws prevented their acquiring even a small farm of their own..."[23] This does not seem to be literally true, but as Presbyterians, their farms would have been getting smaller and smaller. The Penal Laws were known as a "hated set of legal contrivances" that had been designed to convert Catholic Ireland to Protestantism by systematically impoverishing Catholics. One would think that Presbyterians, being very much Protestants, would have benefitted in such a system. But the crown was not satisfied just to steer people into Protestantism; it insisted on

---

[21] Col. Walter H. Parsons Jr., "Churches - Religious Histories," *Brazos County History: Rich Past - Bright Future.* p. 133.

[22] Murray, "Home Life on Early Ranches of Southwest Texas."

[23] Shirlireed Walker, "Community Histories - Towns Past and Present," *Brazos County History*, p. 22.

Anglicanism, and so Presbyterians, who were far more Protestant in character than Anglicans, got the same deal as Catholics under the Penal Laws. It was a stick-and-carrot strategy. The stick was to force Catholics and Presbyterians to divide their land equally between all their male heirs, making the plots smaller with every generation. The carrot was that any son who converted to Anglicanism (Church of Ireland) would inherit all of the father's land. [24]

Scots-Irish who were closer to the edge of poverty would have been bolting from this religious-economic persecution throughout the previous century, pouring into America, especially through Pennsylvania, and carving paths into the wilderness. Because the Henry brothers were nephews of a wealthy squire, and because Bettie, in addition to being a niece of a Parliament member had a father who was a large business owner, we can assume that they were not so close to the edge and therefore simply took longer to reach whatever point of dissatisfaction triggered this radical decision.

In 1800, following an Irish rebellion and brutal suppression by England, the Act of Union was passed, which united England and Scotland with Ireland. This act, which gave us the modern United Kingdom, held out the hope that the Penal Laws at last would be repealed. But two decades had passed and still the Catholics and Presbyterians languished under this apartheid. By 1820, all of them would have lost hope things would ever change. The effects of the failed revolution were lingering too. Some Presbyterian ministers were jailed, and some rebels were offered exile as an alternative to hanging. In some cases whole families were forced to immigrate because of the involvement of one family member in the rebellion of 1798.[25]

The abolition of Irish self-government was another reason for the huge Irish exodus of the nineteenth century. The Henrys were civically aware and politically and

---

[24] "History Of Ireland" www.WesleyJohnston.com

[25] Smith, *American Descendants of James and Margot (O'Hara) Henry*, p iii.

militarily active, as would quickly become evident in the New World, and they would have chafed at foreign rule and second-class status regardless of their declining economic fortunes.[26] Some say the Ulster Presbyterians fled Ireland due to the unjust action of the British Parliament against the wool industry that composed many of their livelihoods.[27]

Additionally, while the Great Potato Famine would not strike for another twenty-five years, Ireland already had suffered a string of lesser famines. In 1816, just five years before the Henrys quit Ireland, the country experienced "the year with no summer." It rained all spring. It snowed in June and July, and heavy cloud cover blotted out the sun. The reason: on April 10 of the previous year, Indonesia's Mount Tambora had exploded in the largest volcanic eruption in recorded history. Its ash encircled the globe creating a nuclear winter. The ensuing famine and associated typhoid epidemic in Ireland killed sixty-five thousand people.

Whatever it was that tipped the scales, the larger reason was that intractable Celtic braid of religious, political, economic, and agricultural woes. But perhaps, leavening all that, the Henrys also were lured in some degree by simple adventure, young people weary of the rainy, pastoral sameness that was their ancestors' world — there and across the Irish Sea in Scotland — back into the mists of prehistory. And if a thirst for adventure was any part of their calculus, they would not be disappointed.

---

[26] http://www.irishtimes.com/ancestor/magazine/emigration/ulster.htm
[27] Smith, *American Descendants*, p. 149.

STAGGERING

3.

A New World

*"Nothing is more wonderful than the art of being free,
but nothing is harder to learn how to use than
freedom."*

—*Alexis de Tocqueville,
Democracy in America, 1835*

IN 1821, THE YEAR FOLLOWING their wedding, they set sail for America with seven other Irish families.[28] The party included Robert's brother William. (Robert was the oldest of four brothers who would eventually immigrate to Texas in the coming years.) The other families included the Fullertons, McMillans, Dunns, Caufields, and Watsons — names that would become increasingly familiar in later years because they continued to sojourn together from place to place and so remain neighbors and due to marriages of children and grandchildren. Of course, they took little with them, but some pitchers and a jar from the Old World stayed in the family for more than a century.[29]

---

[28] Some sources claim it was the day after their wedding.

Tradition holds that the families sailed not from Londonderry Port on the northern coast but from Belfast on northern Ireland's east coast.[30] From Dunn family history, we know that they likely sailed on *The Jane*, an Irish passenger vessel. The Henrys' adventure began sooner than they might have hoped. They had barely nosed out toward sea when a storm rose up that blew them back to port. But the second attempt was successful, and after a grueling crossing that took between six and ten weeks,[31] and during which they endured several more storms, they landed at Charleston, South Carolina.[32] [33] Underscoring the perilous conditions, just five years later, *The Jane* foundered and sank eight miles west of the town of Bude on England's southwestern coast.[34]

Even in a land that already had been criss-crossed and farmed by Europeans for two hundred years, the Irish, with fresh memories of their former tiny plots on tired and worn-out land, must have beheld every part of the New World with wonder — the vast forests, the teeming game, and the dizzying political and economic liberties, freedom of occupation, of assembly, of speech, and of worship.

Within their first year on American soil, Bettie bore their first child, who was given the name of Robert's youngest brother, Hugh. He would be the first of thirteen children born over the next seventeen years, and Bettie called him "my little groundhog."[35] Not much is known about their one-year stay in South Carolina, but they probably moved quickly inland and joined an enclave of other recent Irish

---

[29] Betty Westbrook Trant Family Papers, p. 1.
[30] Betty Westbrook Trant
[31] Smith, American Descendants, p. 149
[32] Pickrell, *Pioneer Women in Texas* p. 163.
[33] Murray, "Home Life on Early Ranches of Southwest Texas."
[34] October 9, 1826. Scheduled Ancient Monument no. 905485. Dunn family history gives the year of immigration as 1820, but agrees with Belfast as the port of departure.
[35] Mrs. Sam Rice, *The Hearne (Texas) Democrat,* February 9, 1967

immigrants.[36]

Who were these people, and what drove them? In his indispensable history of Texas *Lone Star*, T.R. Fehrenbach writes, "The Scots [Irish] landed on the wharves at Philadelphia and Charleston with certain convictions firmly fixed. They were enormously self-disciplined, both by their Puritan ethic and the warlike borderer's life. They had three public virtues: thrift, because they had always been poor and Knox taught poverty was a disgrace; self-reliance, because in the new Reformed world every man felt himself something of an island; and industry, agreeing with St. Paul that who did not work should not eat."[37]

Accordingly, Robert immediately planted a crop of cotton and corn to get them through the year, while Bettie began a crash course in pioneer housekeeping. In an evocative 1940 magazine feature on the Henrys, Myrtle Murray wrote, "As they sat in the soft glow of the pine knots in the huge fireplace built in the center of their first log-room home, they talked about old times in Ireland, the meager news of the community, but most of all, about Texas..."[38]

After harvesting that first crop and having another baby, John,[39] they set a westerly heading for Alabama, caravanning with several other families, many of whom had been with them since Londonderry. When their clothes, bedding, and household essentials were loaded on a covered wagon, Robert gave the command, and with a step by the two "well-broke oxen" the caravan creaked into motion.[40] With

---

[36] Lindsay Hale Boyd, on FindAGrave.com writes: "James Henry's citizenship petition in 1828 gives his home as Chester County, South Carolina, so at least he (and maybe all of them) moved up-river and remained there through 1828.

[37] T.R. Fehrenbach, *Lone Star*, p. 89

[38] Murray, "Home Life on Early Ranches of Southwest Texas."

[39] Records show John D. Henry was born 1822 and died 1846, but mysteriously he does not figure in subsequent stories.

them they carried seed for corn and vegetables and a few chickens and led two milk cows.[41]

Travelers from South Carolina to Alabama would have come along the old Federal Road and along the fall line to Montgomery.[42] The fall line is a geological feature separating coastal plains from uplands, causing every river and stream crossing it to drop with either a waterfall or rapids. Above the fall line, rivers were easier to ford because they were not affected by tides or marshes. Moreover, towns tended to form near falls due to their utility for mills and because cargo boats could go no farther upstream. Fall lines therefore formed natural routes for overland travelers who would resupply in those towns.[43]

Conditions at home in South Carolina had been so primitive that providing for the family on the road was not much different. Cooking with a teakettle and Dutch oven, or "skillet-and-lid," over a campfire was much the same as it had been in their cabin's fireplace, and potatoes were baked in the ashes at night just as before.

The journey was some four hundred fifty miles due west, which if they averaged, being generous, fifteen miles a day would have taken an even month. The "roads" were unimaginably rough, sometimes covered with rocks, often with deep ruts cut in the mud from other wagons. Occasionally, they would have to camp for days while waiting for the roads to dry out before they could continue.

But the hardest part proved to be crossing streams. Bridges were rare sights, and they crossed rivers on "pontoon ferries," large rafts fashioned from logs bound together, floored with rough-hewn boards that were held in place by a cable and pulled across the rivers with ropes.

---

[40] Murray, "Home Life on Early Ranches of Southwest Texas."

[41] Betty Westbrook Trant Family Papers, p. 1.

[42] Richard Denny Parker, *Recollections of Robertson County Texas*, (Salado, Texas: The Anson Jones Press, 1955) p. 15.

[43] Parker, *Roberston County*, p. 15.

In western Alabama's Greene County, they halted the wagon train and made their home for the next seven years, all the while planning their final move into Texas. In this staging area, Robert continued to farm and learn the ways of the New World.

From this period, there are no stories, no vignettes, no details of any kind. But still the record leaves a poignant aftertaste. In the record, we have only three names, and three dates. From these we know that shortly after their arrival in Alabama, in 1824, Bettie had another son, William. He died in infancy. The following year, she had Samuel, who also died in infancy. The next year came little Robert. He too died.

Even for hardened pioneers and stiff-lipped Calvinists, this was a dark time, with crushing grief piled atop crushing labor and untold hardships lost to history. Of course, infant mortality was commonplace. Statistics from the period are unreliable because infant deaths were so under-reported. Our best guesses come from the grim work of latter-day epidemiologists, who step through overgrown cemeteries with clipboards, tallying the small gravestones that are left and dividing their number into the total. It is estimated that on the Western frontier, infant deaths represented half of all deaths. One report puts the death rate for the United States as a whole in 1850 (the earliest year for which there is data) at 22 percent of white babies and 34 percent of black babies.[44] The infant mortality rate in the Henry home now stood at 60 percent.

The causes of the deaths were not recorded. On the frontier, disease was as mysterious as it was numbingly common. As late as 1873, eight children in Leavenworth, Kansas, were buried with the cause of death listed as "teething." But the causes would be common names to us,

---

[44] http://eh.net/encyclopedia/article/haines.demography

and the vast majority now curable: whooping cough, measles, scarlet fever, tuberculosis.[45] Harvey Mitchell, who enters our story sometime later and would become known as the "father of Brazos County," and his wife, Jane, lost their fourth, sixth, seventh, and ninth children as well as one of their grandchildren in one week in January 1870, all to meningitis.[46] What greater grief could ever have been felt by any human soul than that of Harvey and Jane Mitchell during those seven days.

But, of course, there were lots of ways to die on the frontier, and not all microbial. In 1853, when Bettie's and Robert's oldest son, Hugh, was married with children of his own and had settled on his own land close to his parents, he kept a large stock pond just north of his house. His boys had the daily chore of driving the ducks and geese home at evening time from the pond. Their sister Catherine, a toddler, followed the boys home one evening and fell face down into the pond, where she drowned. Hers was the first grave in the Hugh Reed Henry Cemetery.[47]

If you were female, you stood an excellent chance of dying in childbirth, and every labor was an emotional tightrope on which life's greatest joy could tip with the faintest breeze of complication into life's greatest tragedy. You could get thrown from a horse. You could get kicked in the head by a mule, gored by a steer, crushed by a falling tree, nicked by a rusty farm implement, drown in a flood, and of course, simply starve.

BUT AS WITH SO MANY PIONEER FAMILIES, this terrible string of infant deaths was offset by seemingly boundless fertility and virility. In the early nineteenth century, the average American mother had between seven and eight live

---

[45] Charles R. King "Childhood Death: The Health Care of Children on the Kansas Frontier"

[46] Ruth W. Peattis, "Harvey Mitchell" (1821-1901), *Brazos County History*, p. 247.

[47] *Brazos County History*, "The Henry Family," p. 228.

births in her lifetime.[48] Whether it was something in the water or perhaps simply a more faithful adherence to the biblical injunction to be fruitful and multiply, at Staggers Point, most families beat that average handily, having in excess of twelve. Bettie's baker's dozen supports the statistic.[49]

The Henrys surely were susceptible to grief. But whether they were simply made of stiffer stuff than are we or adhered to a theology that more easily absorbed hardship, they moved forward and ever onward in action. According to Fehrenbach, the French historian De Riencourt was "both fascinated and appalled" by the Scots-Irish and wrote of them:

> Strong, inhumanly self-reliant, endowed with an ecstatic dryness of temper which brushed aside the psychological complexities of mysticism, these puritans were geared for a life of action. They shunned objective contemplation and were determined to throw their fanatical energy into this struggle against Nature . . . they fought their own selves with gloomy energy, repressing instincts and emotions, disciplining their entire lives . . . remorselessly brushing aside all men who stood in their path.

To this Fehrenbach concludes: "No Anglo-Celt would have understood the elegant Riencourt. They had no real intention of destroying the Wilderness, or any people who lived in it. Their own sayings were 'God helps them who help themselves,' 'there's no such thing as luck,' and 'Devil take the hindmost,' and they were going West."[50]

---

[48] http://eh.net/encyclopedia/article/haines.demography

[49] Smith, *American Descendants*, p. 270.

[50] Fehrenbach, *Lone Star*, p. 92.

29

By 1829, some eight years after landing in America, the Henrys had become seasoned pioneers and made plans to leave this new nation for the even newer nation of Mexico, which had thrown off Spanish rule only eight years earlier.

Robert applied to empresario Sterling Clack Robertson to become part of the Nashville Company, better known to history as Robertson's Colony, and received his "headright claim" from the Mexican government. Robertson would eventually recruit six hundred families to settle the Brazos River valley in a swath that today encompasses more than thirty counties from Bryan to west of Fort Worth. Over time the colony would be known variously as (in order) the Texas Association, Leftwich's Grant, the Nashville Colony, the Upper Colony, and Robertson's Colony. A tall blond man with a hot temper, a penchant for expensive clothes, and a weakness for the ladies (siring two sons but never marrying), Sterling Robertson was a sometimes bitter rival of Stephen F. Austin, who had already claimed the safer land to the southeast that extended from a long, straight border with Robertson's Colony all the way to the coast and encompassed the mouths of the Brazos and the Colorado.

In 1830, the Mexican government clamped down on American emigration (Imagine the time when Mexico was trying to keep desperate Americans out.), but many Irish likely were welcomed in under the false assumption that they were Catholic. It also is theorized that the Irish immigrants of the early 1830s may have been more acceptable to Mexican authorities than the Scots-Irish who came through the Cumberland Gap earlier, because they would have been less Americanized.[51] If this was truly the Mexicans' rationale, it would prove to be a disastrous miscalculation.

After no doubt much bureaucratic wrangling, the deed from the Mexican government, dated June 1828, was in hand. In the latter part of 1829, it was time to make their

---

[51] Walker, *Brazos County History*, p. 22

long-dreamed-of move.[52] They once again piled everything but their cabin into ox-drawn wagons and started creaking slowly west. Some horses would have been ridden by caravan members while leading still others. As bluestocking Presbyterians, some of the families including the Henrys would not travel on Sunday. Nevertheless, they claimed to have arrived at their destination first "and without any losses."[53]

The Henrys were in the vanguard, some accounts even claiming that Robert was acting as an emissary or scout for the six or seven other families that had crossed from Ireland with them and would arrive in Texas in 1833.

As they rolled through new country west toward Vicksburg or Natchez, Mississippi, Hugh would have been old enough to hold the reins, while John and Katherine, known as "Kitty," likely sat on their mother's lap or jostled along in the wagon behind their parents.

---

[52] There is disagreement in the record about when the Robert Henry family actually moved to Texas. Family papers indicate that it was 1829, and four years before a famous episode fixed at 1833, of which more later. This 1829 date will be used in this narrative going forward. Dixon and Kemp's "Heroes of San Jacinto" (1934) states on p. 408 that they emigrated in November 1834. This assertion seems to be supported by two land grants awarded to Robert dated December 22, 1834, one for one labor and one for 24 labors in Robertson County (McLean, *Papers concerning Robertson's Colony*, Vol. 9, p. 225). However Dixon and Kemp say an 1834 grant to Robert was located in modern Live Oak County, more than 200 miles southeast of Bryan. A document prepared by the Daughters of the Republic of Texas in preparation for the historic marker at the Robert Henry grave states, "The records of Green [sic] County, Alabama show the transfer of property of Robert and Elizabeth Downing Henry in 1832 to John J. Friend for $900.00. A short time after the sale of the property in Alabama, they came to Texas, settling in what is now Robertson County." So we are left with three dates: 1829, 1832, and 1834. One theory that tries to reconcile the first two dates is that Robert came to Texas in 1829 to scout the area for the Irish group then in Alabama, returned, sold his property, and moved the family in 1832. Another theory might be that the family moved in 1829 but sold its Alabama property three years later after they saw that things might work out in the new country. As for the 1834 date, this seems too late and would make subsequent timeline that has been passed down by the family impossible. What is more, many families moved first and received their land grants months or even years later.

[53] Murray, "Home Life on Early Ranches of Southwest Texas."

The young family must have thought it was approaching the Pacific Ocean when at last the Mississippi River came into view. Much too deep to ford and much too wide for ferries, it had to be crossed, one party at a time, by steam-driven paddle boats. Robert and the other men helped load the ferry, coaxing his oxen and wagon carefully onto the steamboat while Bettie kept a firm hold on the children. When they were all aboard, the oxen were loosened from the wagon and everything securely fastened.

The captain told all aboard not to be scared, adding "I've never lost a soul." But Bettie held the children tightly nonetheless as the muddy whitecaps lapped at the steamboat's bulwarks. A shrill whistle from the captain and the boat pulled away, leaving yet another world behind. It took many hours for the whole caravan to cross.

They continued slowly west, now through the swamps and river bottoms of Louisiana. When they crossed the Sabine River, probably at Gaines Ferry, they had arrived in Texas. Looking nothing like the pastureland they had envisioned, they might have looked to the locals for some reassurance that they were on the right path. And from Natchez to Natchitoches to Nacogdoches, their Irish tongues were getting an exotic workout. They now followed the Old San Antonio Road or El Camino Real. With many streams but just a few more major rivers to cross, they were determined to make it to "the prairie near the Brazos."

4.

Home - The Claypan

"... each one can imagine for himself what could happen in a land so strange and so poor and so lacking in every single thing that it seemed impossible either to be in it or to escape from it."

—Alvar Nunez Cabeza de Vaca,
on landing in Texas in 1542

"This extensive undulating section is probably as desirable a country for residence of man as any upon the face of the earth."

—Mary Austin Holley, Sister of Stephen F. Austin[54]

FOR ALL INTENTS AND PURPOSES, the East Texas town of Nacogdoches was the edge of civilization, and every day they traveled beyond it was a day more dangerous than the last. Two days beyond Nacogdoches they came to the Angelina River, which was fordable. They passed a Delaware Indian village and continued to the southwest past a Neches Indian village. The following day they would have passed the ruins

---

[54] Parker, *Recollections of Robertson County*, p. 3.

of the Spanish mission called San Francisco de los Tejas, a grim reminder of the failure of the Spanish to subdue this vast territory in the name of either the crown or the cross. They traversed the Trinity probably at Robbins' Ferry, and days later, entered the Brazos watershed and crossed the Navasota.

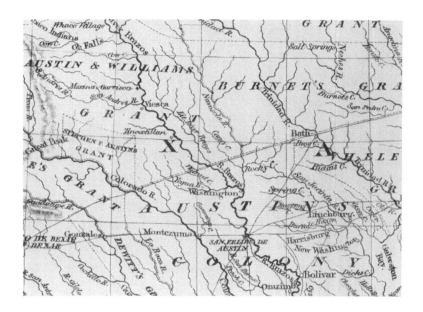

Detail of 1841 Map of Texas Showing Brazos River system and Old San Antonio Road. Staggers Point was just northeast of where the OSR crosses the Little Brazos River, in the center of the image, just inside modern Robertson County.

Finally, a day beyond the Navasota and after a westward journey of some six hundred miles, which probably had taken between six weeks and two months, the oxen train pulled off the road to camp under a large pecan tree. The Henrys had reached their "headright league." That night, they heard both wolves and panthers coming near their camp, dispelling any illusions they might have still harbored of Texas as paradise. It was a land of danger, but also of plenty. Little did they expect that the nuts from that pecan tree would continue to feed the family for six generations.[55]

The next morning, they went on a little farther, turned north off the Old San Antonio Road, and after just one or two miles arrived at their homesite on the banks of the Little Brazos River, a seventy-mile tributary just east of the Brazos. Robert chose a location fronting the river to have a sufficient and permanent supply of water. The nearest modern town is Benchley. The thrill of surveying their very own, very large parcel of land must have been tempered by the realization that their nearest neighbor was eight miles away.[56]

The very first order of business would have been to form a makeshift corral so that the oxen and horses could be let out of their hobbles or off the picket lines to which they had been tethered at every stop along their journey. Finding a grassy clearing for them to graze, Bettie, Robert, and the older children might have begun by dragging dead branches into a circle. For the family, Robert might have fashioned a crude tent of canvas over poles, or they might have simply continued to sleep in the covered wagons while Robert set about building his third log cabin since arriving in North America.

The makeshift corral would as soon as possible have been replaced with a split-rail fence, in which logs about eight feet long were split into quarters and the rails laid in a self-supporting cross-hatch pattern to form the perimeter. Though the zig-zag of the fence used more wood, it had the advantage of being constructible without hardware or digging, and so could be moved with relative ease.

When it came time to build their home, Robert would find and fell straight post oaks with his axe, and after hacking off their branches he would have then used the

---

[55] Jimmie Henry Rice, *The Hearne Democrat*, September 19, 1968.

[56] Murray, "Home Life on Early Ranches of Southwest Texas."

horses or oxen to drag them to the building site. He'd then set about the exhausting work of splitting the logs with axes, sledges and iron splitting wedges. The straight edges were then hewn as smooth as possible before the logs were laid tightly side-by-side, flat edges up, to form the cabin's foundation and "puncheon" floor.

After the floor, it was up and up with logs around, notching and dovetailing them at the corners. A rock fireplace and chimney was the soul of the house, the place in which they would cook and around which they would huddle during cold winter evenings. The roof was vaulted with smaller poles, and shingles split out with a froe and club and, if nails were not available, weighed down with branches or rocks. Windows were cut after construction, and the cracks between the logs were chinked with a mixture of clay and straw, which the Scots-Irish called "catin clay" (or sometimes "cat-and-clay").[57]

It is written that "between 1829 and 1834, the Irish immigrants preferred the woods to the black prairie because they needed easy access to timber for homes and rail fences. It also afforded better hiding places from the Indians."[58] The soil was rich in the river bottom. The mesquite grass and wild rye were two to three feet high, ready for the grinding teeth of horses and cattle. Sometime later, this area became known as Rye Community. Some say it was so named for the patch of rye grown from seed that Robert brought with him from Ireland, but rye grew wild as well. While the Henrys tried to use some of the rye for bread, Bettie could make better bread from sweet potatoes. There were abundant wild onions, wild plums and berries, and they later raised peaches and a garden. But the first year was hard, and they had to replant the corn, which used up most of their supply of seedcorn. With the milk cows and chicken eggs, they scraped by.[59]

---

[57] Michael Montgomery, *From Ulster to America: The Scotch-Irish Heritage of American English*, (Belfast: Ulster Historical Foundation, 2006) p. 34.

[58] Henry, "The Henry Family," *Brazos County History*, p. 226.

The area where the Henrys and the other Staggers Point settlers would make their home for generations to come straddles two modern Texas counties: Brazos, named for the river that forms the county's western border, and above it, Robertson, named for the empresario. The settlers moved around but generally stayed between the Brazos on the west and the Navasota on the east. South of Bryan, the latter empties to the former, forming Brazos County into a rough, southeast-pointing triangle.

East-central Texas is hard to conjure because it does not fit neatly into any of Texas' iconic regions. It is well east of the rocky Texas Hill Country that most think of as "Central Texas" but west of the piney woods that dominate East Texas. Instead it is mash-up, a land of constant variety. Hilltops are prairie dotted with clusters of oaks. The shallow valleys separating the hills are lush with hardwood forests, while the river and stream bottoms are jungles of trees, vines, and cane. Bettie and Robert would have noted all of this variety within the space of a few miles around their claim, if not from acre to acre. Here, the black prairie of north Texas is gerrymandered with the Post Oak Belt, which in turn might host a stray stand of pines wandering in from the east, coastal prairie species like mesquite and prickly pear cactus from the south and west, and all of it permeated by arteries of riparian jungles growing in ancient alluvial soils for miles along the river bottoms. In total, the region is known as "the Claypan" because of a layer of clay sitting a few feet below the sandy surface that slows the rainwater on its voyage underground.

An interesting description of the Brazos River bottom in 1831 was left by a traveler known only as "Fiske." He described how the cane breaks occasionally would "form one thick growth, impenetrable when the cane is dry and hard. The frequent passage of men and horses keeps open a narrow

---

[59] Betty Westbrook Trant Family Papers, p. 1.

path, not wide enough for two mustangs to pass with convenience. The reeds grow to the height of about twenty feet, and are so slender, that having no support directly from the path, they droop a little inward, and so meet and intermingle their tops, forming a complete covering overhead."[60] With its fenced-off ranches, farms, and subdivisions, the area of course appears quite different today, but one can still note all these features on a casual tour.

Much more notably different now than the land is the wildlife. By all accounts, and as is the case virtually anywhere in America, the game then was both more abundant and more diverse. There were teeming deer, of course, but also bison, which in that day were so abundant on the open plains to the northwest that herds of them easily could have been seen from space — herds ten miles wide by one hundred ten miles long.[61] Throughout the nineteenth century this area supported apex predators including black bear, panthers, and gray wolves, which were described as a subtype that sported longer hair around the head and shoulders like a lion's mane.

The forest hosted three kinds of large feral mammals, all courtesy of the Spanish: wild longhorn cattle, which many settlers assumed to be indigenous instead of the invasive exotics they were. It was said the cattle were wilder and more skittish than the deer. Droves of wild hogs roamed the woods, as they do still in ever-increasing numbers. And even mustangs ran in the forests and over the prairies in herds the settlers called "cavayards." Soon after arriving at the Little Brazos, Robert rode out onto Cedar Prairie, captured the colt of a wild mare, and when it was grown bred it to some of the horses he had brought with him from Alabama, a practice he would repeat in years to come.

On the wing, there were huge flocks of turkeys, which

---

[60] LifeontheBrazos.com

[61] Gwynn, *Empire of the Summer Moon*

"had to be shot low because they were so fat that when they fell to earth from any height their breasts would burst open."[62]

Years later Robert's youngest brother, Hugh, became the last of the four Henry brothers to arrive in Texas. Unlike the others, he came through Galveston, then to Houston, then to Boonville, the county seat, by ox-wagon. He finished his journey on foot to brother James' house, which took him through a thickly wooded area. On the hike he saw a turtle for the first time ever on land. He picked it up and wrapped it in his handkerchief. When he arrived at James' home, he reportedly said, "And beglorie, Jimmy, oi've found the queerest frog you ever saw!"

"Why that's just an old land terrapin," James replied, "but why did you wrap it in your kerchief?"

Hugh said, "Well dom my soul, Jimmy, I was afraid the critter would crawl out of its house."[63]

Short of a description of this virgin area from Bettie's or Robert's own hand, the best we can do is from William Dewees, who, in a letter to a friend back in his home of Kentucky, describes east-central Texas as it appeared seven years earlier:

Brazos River, Coahuila and Texas, July, 16, 1822

Dear Friend – After a long and toilsome journey I arrived at this point from Red river, in company with three or four families from that country, on the first day of January, last. We encamped at the crossing of the old San Antonio road, two miles above the mouth of the Little Brazos river. We were several months in getting here, there being several families in company,

---

[62] Murray, "Home Life on Early Ranches of Southwest Texas."

[63] Henry, "The Henry Family," *Brazos County History,* p. 231.

among whom were quite a number of women and children. A part of the time we were detained by the sickness of one or another of the company, besides this, we lost several horses on the way, and in fact we seemed to meet with a great many misfortunes. We carried our luggage entirely upon pack-horses, the roads being perfectly impassable for a vehicle of any description. I believe I have already given you a description of the country, between Pecan Point and Nacogdoches, in a former letter. From the latter place to the Brazos the county is high and dry; the land is generally poor, though well timbered between Nacogdoches and the Trinity, from there on, we met with large prairies. On arriving at the Brazos we found two families, Garrett and Hibbings, who had got there a few days before us, and were engaged in erecting cabins. We were, all of us, much pleased with the situation of this place, and decided to remain here for the present. The settlement now consisted of seven families; there is no other settlement within fifty miles. About the time of our arrival here, a few families settled below us on this river, near the old La Bahia crossing.

As far as we have seen, we are well pleased with this part of the country. As high up as we have explored, the Brazos has the appearance of being a large navigable river. The land is very rich and fertile! The timber is good, and in places, particularly on Little river, the white oak and cedar reminds me very forcibly of the timber in Kentucky.

Our mode of living, particularly for the women and children, has been a rough one since our arrival on this river. About that time our bread-stuff gave out, and we had no chance of obtaining more till we could raise it, and we have been obliged to subsist entirely upon the game which we take in the woods and prairies. We have no reason to fear suffering for food, as the country is literally alive with all kinds of game. We have only to go out for a few miles into a swamp between the Big and Little Brazos, to find as many wild cattle as one could wish. If we desire buffalo meat, we are able to go out, load our horses, and return the same day. Bears are very plenty, but we are obliged to use great care when hunting for them, lest the havalenas (meaning the peccary) kill our dogs.

The families have saved a few pecks of corn which we planted, but on account of the dry weather and the want of culture, it will yield but a small amount.

The only cows we have, are a few which were brought out by Cherokee John Williams. This of course will prove a good stock country, for the prairies are teeming with wild horses and cattle. There are a vast quantity of bee trees about here, so that we have no want of honey; one might almost give this country the same description as was anciently given of Canaan, "a land flowing with milk and honey," but we are rather short off for the milk just now.

Upon the whole we spend our time very pleasantly; when we get tired of lying about camp, we mend up our moccasins, and start up the Brazos hunting buffalo, more for pastime than for anything else. We frequently are gone out for two or three weeks; we generally go up as high as we dare go, on account of the Whaco Indians. You would scarcely believe me, were I to tell you of the vast herds of buffalo which abound here; I have frequently seen a thousand in a day between this place and the mouth of Little river.

In May, some six or seven of us took a trip as high up as Little river by water. We constructed a small canoe, and about the time we were ready to start, a young gentleman, who had just arrived here from the States, desired to make the trip with us. To this we consented. On our way, we would amuse ourselves by going out and shooting wild cattle, which are in great abundance here. It was dangerous for us to encamp at night, on the east side of the river, on account of the cattle coming in for water, the night being the only time they go to water. We made our station camp at the mouth of Little river on the beach! There we stayed two weeks, killing and drying buffalo meat. We went out every day, killed a buffalo or two apiece, and brought the choice pieces, particularly the tongues, into camp. Our young friend, whom I mentioned as having just come out from the States, had informed me that he was a minister of the gospel. When one kills a buffalo, he generally lays claim to the tongue as private property, it being a very choice piece; the other portions are shared equally. Our little yankee preacher seemed to enjoy himself very well during the trip, though he was greatly disturbed by our profanity, for we were a rough set. My reason for calling him a yankee, by the by, is on account of the way he managed to get our buffalo tongues. About the time we got our canoe loaded with meat ready to start home, he proposed a plan to break us from swearing, to which we all very readily agreed. The first one who used an oath, was to give whoever first reminded him of it, one of his dried buffalo tongues. Oaths being so common with us, we, of course, did not notice them, and in less than three days, the minister was possessor of our dried tongues.

Perhaps a description of the wild rye, which grows very plentifully here in the bottoms, might not be uninteresting to you. Indeed, I know if I can give you half an idea of its beauty, you cannot fail to be delighted. The bottom of the Brazos is very wide and level, and in the summer season, rye grows here spontaneously, about four feet high. It would, were it not for the timber standing in the midst, present the same appearance which a cultivated rye field in the States presents, for miles and miles. In fact, it far surpasses the common rye fields in beauty, being much larger and thicker.

I have never witnessed a sight of the kind, which, in my opinion, was more beautiful than this. The color of it is far deeper and richer than any grain I have ever before seen. I always admired the sight of a fine wheat field at home, but when I look at this, I sometimes wonder how I could ever have thought that beautiful; it seems so insignificant when compared with this rye. The timber, in the midst of which it grows, renders the sight the more imposing. There is not in these wild rye bottoms any undergrowth to the timber. The trees are large and tall! The long moss waves from their thick branches, and mixes with the heads of the rye; all seems still, solemn and beautiful, beyond the power of pen to describe. One must see it to get even a faint idea of its beauty.

You, in Kentucky, cannot for a moment conceive of the beauty of one of our prairies in the spring. Imagine for yourself a vast plain extending as far as the eye can reach, with nothing but the deep blue sky to bound the prospect, excepting on the east side where runs a broad red stream, with lofty trees rearing themselves upon its banks, and you have our prairie. This is covered with a carpet of the richest verdure, from the midst of which spring up wild flowers of every hue and shade, rendering the scene one of almost fairy-like beauty. Indeed, it is impossible to step without crushing these fairest of nature's works. Upon these natural flower gardens feed numerous herds of buffalo, deer, and other wild animals. Here and there may be seen beautiful clumps of trees, and anon, a little thicket comes in view. The flowers of the prairie are certainly the most beautiful which I have ever beheld. Our ladies in Kentucky would feel themselves amply repaid for all the labor, which they bestow upon their beautiful flower gardens, could they but afford one half of the beauty of one of our prairies.

Yours truly, W. B. D.

[William B. Dewees][64]

Above the banks of the Little Brazos, in these fields of wild rye and mesquite grass, Robert and Bettie pastured their own cattle, the biggest risk being these cattle falling in with their wild cousins and wandering off for good, a bovine *Call of the Wild*.[65] Their own hogs were allowed to fatten up by grazing loose among the post oak acorns or "mast."

BEING AT THE LEADING EDGE of this movement of settlers presented special challenges, to put it mildly. Most accounts of the time are probably three hundred percent too romantic. While some writers paint a gauzy picture of Bettie and the children galloping over the flowering prairies while Robert happily notched the logs of their cabin, Noah Smithwick offered a perhaps more realistic portrait:

Men talked hopefully of the future; children reveled in the novelty of the present; but the

---

[64] Dewees, W.B. *Letters from an Early Settler of Texas.* (Louisville, KY: Morton & Griswold, 1852), pp. 23-28.

[65] Jim Boyd, *Grandfather's Journal: The Record of the First Seale Family in Texas,* (Indiatlantic, Fla.: Self-published, 2003).

women — ah, there was where the situation bore heaviest. As one old lady remarked, Texas was 'a heaven for men and dogs, but a hell for women and oxen.' They — the women — talked sadly of the old homes and friends left behind, so very far behind it seemed then, of the hardships and bitter privations they were undergoing and the dangers that surrounded them. They had not even the solace of constant employment. The spinning wheel and loom had been left behind. There was, as yet, no use for them — there was nothing to spin. There was no house to keep in order; the meager fare was so simple as to require little time for its preparation. There was no poultry, no dairy, no garden, no books, or papers as nowadays — and, if there had been, many of them could not read — no schools, no churches — nothing to break the dull monotony of their lives, save an occasional wrangle among the children and dogs. The men at least had the excitement of killing game and cutting bee trees.[66]

There is reason to believe the Henrys and their ilk did not allow the above situation to persist very long, and soon enough all of those elements of "employment" were established with a vengeance. The hardships notwithstanding, for the next four years they lived among east-central Texas' abundance in relative peace, harvesting and harnessing it however they could. But they were about to find out why land here was free for the asking.

It is widely accepted that the Mexicans' chief motivation for recruiting Anglo colonists was to create a buffer on their

---

[66] Eugene Barker, *Texas History For High Schools and Colleges*, (Dallas: The Southwest Press, 1929) p. 142.

northern frontier to absorb the Indians' violence, especially the Comanche. Insofar as this cynical motive is true, Mexico's near immediate loss of Texas to those Anglo settlers presents a bit of poetic justice. Some say the natives were not so hostile to the settlers at first, but that the Mexicans, concluding that the Anglos were more dangerous to their cause than the Indians they were recruited to deflect, turned the tables and incited the Indians to hostility toward the Anglos. This was definitely true in the aftermath of the Texas Revolution, when conspiratorial communications between Mexicans and Cherokees were intercepted. Whether this was also true pre-revolution or whether the Indians themselves saw the settlers as a threat — rightly — or simply an easy target, trouble with Indians was growing.

5.

The Lord and I Will Take
the Children

ONE SIGN INDIAN TROUBLE WAS GROWING can be seen in how the Henrys worshipped. It had been eight years since they had left Ireland, but once again they were being persecuted for their religion. Because the Mexican constitution of 1824 outlawed all religions except Roman Catholicism, the Henrys held services for the settlement in their cabin.[67] But they had to hold two services because half of the members would pray while the other half kept watch for Indians, then they would switch.[68]

Robert and Bettie had big plans for the farm, but if their livestock was in constant danger of being stolen, then their livelihood was too. More to the point, if the family was in constant danger of being killed, then their entire gamble from Londonderry on would have been for naught.

Anne Sutherland writes, "In a number of spectacular

---

[67] Col. Walter H. Parsons Jr. "Religion in Brazos County," *Brazos County History*, p. 133.
[68] Pickrell, *Pioneer Women of Texas*

raids in which hundreds and hundreds of Comanche warriors swept into the area, whole families and settlements in Robertson's Colony were wiped out, survivors fleeing east to Nacogdoches for safety."[69]

Fear gripped the land. The unceasing attacks caused the Irish immigrant James Dunn, who lived just east of Staggers Point, to use ten-foot cedar logs and sod to enclose a three-acre parcel of land and convert his cabin into a two-story blockhouse fort, known to history as Dunn's Fort.[70] It had also caused the Mexicans in 1830 to build a fort a few miles to the west on the Brazos River, giving it a name that pops off modern maps like a befeathered Aztec warrior standing in a crowd of leather-clad cowboys: Tenoxtitlan.

So Robert became a minuteman, a sort of forerunner of the Texas Rangers. There was no formal organization in which he enlisted but rather a rag-tag group of settlers who pursued the natives in the name of safer territory. Nothing was surgical about this activity. "Indians" were attacking settlers, so settlers went after "Indians." Were the targets always the guilty party? Certainly not, but settlers were in an impossible moral situation in relation to Indians. Defense, preemption, revenge, and racism became hopelessly tangled, and few saw the point in untangling them. Frontier life was guerilla warfare in which the Indians initially held all the cards, and being able to tell enemy combatants from the indigenous population was impossible, just as it proved to be in Vietnam, in Iraq, and anywhere else where a military collision is overlaid with racial and cultural identity. The natives were maddeningly mobile, preternaturally stealthy, and ruthless in ways the settlers never fully replicated though some would try. Over the coming decades, the conflict would devolve into a mutual genocide.

---

[69] Anne H. Sutherland, *The Robertsons, the Sutherlands, and the Making of Texas*, (College Station: Texas A&M Press, 2006). p. 85.

[70] *The Bryan Daily Eagle*, August 28, 1960.

One episode in particular illustrates the hardship created for the mothers when the fathers took the fight to the Indians. Robert's brother William too became a minuteman. Once while William was off pursuing Indians, his wife, Mary Fullerton Henry, decided to milk the cow just before dark. When she opened the door, she saw an object bobbing up and down near the old rail cowpen. "My God! It's Indians!" she cried, and barred herself and the children in the house. There they sat huddled together and hungry for the entire night, not daring to make a peep. Normally, the most frightening sounds of the night were the wolves digging underneath their puncheon-log floors, but she barely noticed the digging that night as all her attention was tuned to listening for the blood-curdling war cries that signaled an Indian attack.

Daylight came, and the children were now unbearably hungry. She decided they must have milk. With a pounding heart she opened the cabin door, and to her horror, there was the brown face, still moving by the cowpen. She froze, and studied it. It was nothing but her old milk gourd swinging in the breeze on the weed by which she had hung it. Such was the fear of Indians that even wolves came a distant second.[71]

LITTLE DID EITHER SIDE in this conflict suspect how closely they were related to the other. It is odd to think that some thirty-thousand years earlier, there was a man, probably in or near Kazakhstan, who had two sons. One of them moved a few miles to the east, the other a few to the west. They started their own families and continued to follow game in opposite directions. The westering family eventually moved into Europe, and a branch of the eastering family eventually crossed the Bering land bridge and populated the New World all the way to Tierra del Fuego. Descendants of the western son eventually crossed the Atlantic and clashed with

---

[71] Galloway, Briggs, and Hicks, "Mary Fullerton Henry Dixon," *The Irish of Staggers Point*, p. 23.

descendants of the eastern son, each having half-circled the globe in opposite directions. And though they appeared as different to each other as to be different species, in fact population geneticists now know with certainty that these clashing civilizations were cousins separated from that Kazakh father, carrier of the M45 genetic marker, by merely one thousand generations.

In the final analysis, these two cultures were simply incompatible — one based on settling and private property; the other based just as fundamentally on constant movement. (While it's quite true that many Indians did settle, and that many whites moved around, the greatest flashpoints of the ongoing conflict were between whites who settled and Indians who did not. And when Indians did settle, it was as a collective, with a much looser sense of individual private property.) One society was based on Victorian values — imperialist, entitled, self-congratulatory. The other literally was Stone Age, with attendant belief in magic and heavy emphasis on taboos. One was organized with a complex vertical hierarchy that integrated millions of people. The other was composed of hundreds of autonomous societies, each with a shallow horizontal authority structure.

One culture possessed a burgeoning sense of universal rights — however wanting; the other operated with a worldview completely dominated by tribal allegiance and alliances: if it benefited the tribe, it was by definition good. Through this lens, this logic, the terrorism of massacres is virtuous if it benefits the tribe, the more terrifying, the more virtuous. Of course, in no way was this unique to American Indians; many human societies have passed through this stage of development and many have yet to. Leopold's Congo of the 1890s; Hitler's Germany of the 1930s; Mugabe's Zimbabwe exists still. In some degree or another, in-group/out-group worldview is the kernel of all human conflict, a nut we have only now begun to crack.

In 1889, when Indian wars had finally drawn to a close, John Wilbarger published a book called simply *Indian*

Depredations in Texas. In it he devotes more than six hundred seventy pages to detailing massacres and sometimes the chases and battles that ensued. Mind you, these were just in Texas, between 1820 and about 1880. (The book's accuracy has come under much criticism by scholars, but even if half its episodes were fantasy, it still gives one a sobering reminder about the scale of the conflict.) Wilbarger, who was a Methodist minister, expressed sentiments that are instructive both because they were so jaw-droppingly racist and because they were so commonly held. (Below, "Lo" is a reference to Alexander Pope's poem "Essay on Man," a famous exponent of the "noble savage" idea.)

> In our opinion, the aborigines of the American continent, pure and simple, were all naturally incapable of progress, and that their existence was only intended to be a temporary one, and that it should cease as soon as their places could be filled by a progressive people, such as the Anglo-Saxon race. The 'old Texans' have not unfrequently [sic] been censured by some of the maudlin, sentimental writers before referred to for having treated poor Lo in a few isolated cases in a barbarous manner. Such writers probably never saw a wild Indian in their lives — never had their fathers, mothers, brothers or sisters butchered by them in cold blood; never had their little sons and daughters carried away by them into captivity, to be brought up as savages, and taught to believe that robbery was meritorious, and cold blooded murder a praiseworthy act, and certainly they never themselves had their own limbs beaten, bruised, burnt and tortured with fiendish ingenuity by 'ye gentle savages,' nor their scalps ruthlessly torn from their bleeding heads, for if the latter experience had been

51

theirs, and they had survived the pleasant operation (as some have done in Texas) we are inclined to think the exposure of their naked skulls to the influences of wind and weather might have so softened them as to permit the entrance of a little common sense. ... Nevertheless, we are glad he is gone, and that there are no Indians now in Texas except 'good ones,' who are as dead as Julius Caesar.[72]

Not surprisingly given this tone and the boundless hatred Wilbarger held for his subject, we find out on the very next page that his own brother had been scalped and left for dead in what is now a lovely park in east Austin called Pecan Springs. (Incredibly, Josiah Wilbarger lived another eleven years without a scalp, his skull slowly wearing away, before accidentally hitting his head on a low doorway and dying soon after.) If modern Texans can be grateful for anything, it is that they do not have to live with this conflict, one that makes the American struggle with international terrorism seem positively quaint and our urban violence seem like schoolyard shenanigans. Though Texas' brief and successful revolt from Mexico was what captured America's imagination, the conflict that really shaped Texas' civic geography was the glacial, grinding Indian war. And more blood was spilled in Texas between Indians and whites than anywhere else on the continent.[73]

To further understand the extent of the animosity of Anglos toward their co-inhabitants we need only look at the language of the best friend the Indians ever had in Texas, Sam Houston:

If you wish to reconciliate the Indians, the

---

[72] J.W. Wilbarger, *Indian Depredations in Texas*, (Austin: Hutchings Printing House, 1889), p. 6.

[73] Fehrenbach, *Lone Star*.

way is open for it. He is really in a state of
tutelage. He is not as intelligent as the white
man. He has not the arts of civilization around
him. He has his savage nature. He has
associations and influences which operate on
him, and lead him to a state of war by way of
excitement or employment. But sir, if you
wish to make peace with the Indians, there is
one fundamental principle which you must
observe, and then you will reconciliate him:
that is, to extend to him strict justice, to do
him no wrong, to violate none of his rights. Do
this, and you will make the Indian your
friend. When you have once inspired him with
confidence and secured his friendship, it is
easy to lead him in the paths of civilization
and improvement.[74]

—"Concerning the Best Methods of
Controlling Indians,"
Remarks in the United States Senate,
January 31, 1857

That this mixture of true and false assertions was the
best any Anglo said of them helps us frame the mindset of
the time even more accurately.

In 1899, Noah Smithwick reflected on his sojourns in
Texas during those early years. Smithwick spent three
months among the Comanches, and much of what we know
about their daily life was conveyed in his memoir. Smithwick
was a quintessential man of his era, that is to say, not
sentimental about much of anything. But in his winter, he
showed an admirable complexity of thought on the matter of
the Texas Indians:

---

[74] *The Writings of Sam Houston,* Ed. Amelia W. Williams and Eugene C.
Barker, (Austin: University of Texas Press, 1941), p. 411.

I had many long, earnest talks with those old Comanche chiefs, and I could not but admit the justice of their contention. The country they considered theirs by the right of inheritance; the game had been placed there for their food... Before the advent of the white man the Indians held full sway. They drove out the Spanish missionaries who attempted to take possession of the country as they had done in Mexico and California, and inspired the Mexicans with such a holy horror of them that they (the Indians) went into the Mexican towns and helped themselves to whatever they wanted, no one daring to oppose them. They tried that game on the Americans, and to their dismay found it would not work. Then, too, the northern Indians came among them, telling how they had been despoiled of their homes and hunting grounds by the pale face, and warning the Texas Indians that it would be the same in their case. They were becoming uneasy and wanted some kind of an agreement by which their hunting grounds would be secured to them. I really felt mean and almost ashamed of belonging to the superior race when listening to the recital of wrongs the redmen had suffered at the hands of my people.

"Almost." It seems no Anglo settler no matter how progressive could make it through a statement on Indians without some reference to the inherent superiority of whites. Smithwick concludes, saying that despite his pangs of conscience, "Nevertheless, when they made hostile incursions into the settlements I joined in the pursuit and hunted them as mercilessly as any one."[75]

As a minuteman, Robert had to have a bag of moulded bullets ready, his horse near enough to be saddled at a moment's notice, and the ability go wherever needed. When he left, he and Bettie both knew there was a decent chance he would not come back. Bettie was often left alone for long stretches with the children, in charge of the crops and in care of the cattle they were beginning to accumulate. She moulded bullets to be ready for Robert whenever he returned. And she probably used a few herself. As one historian writes, "The women were well trained and many were expert shots with rifles, which posed an advantage as bands of horse thieves would raid the farms."[76]

The men would stay gone so long it is said that when the fathers returned home from chasing Indians, their own children would not recognize them from the length of their hair and beards.

But even as Robert hunted the Indians to protect the settlement, Bettie and the children apparently knew some of Texas' native people and had a positive relationship with them. When Bettie had Elizabeth in 1833, a group of native women came to see her and brought her presents. One of them had no present so she gave her "a drink of honey."[77] They were probably Tonkawa, Waco, or Tawakoni, the local tribes of the area.[78] This episode is a tantalizing bit of incongruity that leaves us wondering and wanting more, but we are left to speculate. The friendship might have been the result of Bettie's role as a folk-doctor and midwife to the community, of which more later. One account says, "She always expressed a friendliness for the Indians, but held a strong feeling of fear for the Mexicans."[79] Whatever that

[75] Smithwick, *Evolution of a State*, p. 189.

[76] Henry, "The Henry Family," *Brazos County History*, p. 226.

[77] Murray, "Home Life on Early Ranches of Southwest Texas."

[78] Parker, *Recollections of Robertson County*, p. 5.

[79] Betty Westbrook Trant Family Papers, p. 1

relationship was like, within a few weeks of this touching bicultural baby shower, Bettie would no longer be a resident of Staggers Point.

On October 19, 1833, a rider came through reporting that Comanches had killed several settlers on Yegua Creek, another tributary of the Brazos a short distance west, had stolen most of their horses and virtually all of their cattle, and were headed for Staggers Point.[80]

We have no corroboration of this massacre, but many such events would have gone unreported, especially during these earliest years of settlement when newspapers were few, far between, and short-lived. The closest report to the time and place is the aforementioned scalping of Josiah Wilbarger, which occurred just two months earlier and in the right direction (Austin) albeit twice as far away as any part of the Yegua.

At Staggers Point, Robert had become leader of the minutemen, and they had resolved to go on the offensive. The night before leaving home, he told Bettie, "If I had the time, I could carry you over to the fort at Nacogdoches, where you could stay in safety until I come for you, but I can't get off. I'm bound to go with the company early in the morning."

"Robert Henry, we are Christians, aren't we?" she replied.

Not satisfied with that general a distinction, he volleyed, "We are Presbyterians, aren't we?"

"Yes. The Presbyterians believe they are God's very own, don't they?" Bettie asked.

"Yes."

"Do you believe it?" she pressed.

"We certainly do," he answered.

---

[80] Ann Melvin, "Getting in Touch with Texas Roots," *Dallas Morning News*, Fall 1986.

"Give me your hand on it." They clasped hands and embraced each other, knelt, and prayed. When they arose, she was the first to speak: "Robert Henry, let us be up early in the morning so that you will be ready to join the company when they are ready to start.[81] Bob, the Lord and I will take the children to the fort at Nacogdoches, and we will be there waiting for you when you come for us."[82]

In the morning, Robert mustered the minutemen and set out to the west in pursuit of the Comanches.[83] Bettie hurriedly jerry-rigged the crude plow gear into a hitch and greased an old wagon that had been used mostly behind oxen. On it she loaded most of their clothes, ropes, and axes. But this journey required speed more than power. So she left the oxen and instead hitched two gentle ponies to it. A third pack horse would follow behind. Lastly, she loaded in her sidesaddle, what provisions she had — mostly dried bison — and finally, four of her children, the youngest, Elizabeth, just eleven weeks old.

As fast as she could, she started out on the one hundred fifty-mile journey northeast along the Old San Antonio Road, the wagon trail by which they had reached their claim. This ancient road was already one hundred forty-two years old — blazed in 1691 by the first provincial Spanish governor of Texas, Don Domingo Teran de los Rios. Because it was ordered by the King of Spain, it was then known as El

---

81 Burkhart, "Pioneer Ancestors"

82 Henry, "The Henry Family," *Brazos County History,* p. 227.

83 Several accounts of this story, including the Daughters of the Republic of Texas background document for Robert Henry's historical marker (p.3), state that it was Mexicans who were in pursuit, not Comanches. The author believes it was Comanches and not Mexicans because of the heavy preponderance of retellings that say they were Indians and because so many other elements of the story comport with Indian violence and minutemen action of the time. Most compelling of all is the fact that A.W. Buchanan, who heard the story from Bettie herself, says they were Indians in his 1932 *Bryan Eagle* remembrance. Mexicans might have been mistakenly introduced into story due to conflation with stories of the Runaway Scrape, during which thousands of settlers fled east under similar conditions when word came that the Mexican Army was advancing into Texas.

Camino Real. But "royal highway" was overselling it, even then. The Old San Antonio Road, whose historic path is traced today roughly by Texas State Highway 21, was really just a network of wagon-rutted paths through the forests and across the prairies, with trails peeling off and merging again as it passed rag-tag settlements. It is known variously as El Camino Real, the Old San Antonio Road, the Old Spanish Road, the Bexar-Nacogdoches Road, the Nacogdoches Road, and so forth. This segment was part of a Spanish road system that once stretched from Mexico City to Florida.

Not every immigrant to 1830s Texas shared the Henrys' God-fearing and hard-working way of life. Bettie reported that the road was full of travelers of every description, including "all sorts of marauders, bandits, and cut-throats."[84] Indeed, the area that would become Brazos County in time would develop quite a rough reputation. For every family like the Henrys who were importing Puritan values, there were probably two or three men — always men — running from the law, from creditors, or from other personal failures somewhere in a past life to the east. The race track that would soon be built near Staggers Point would not exactly help matters.

In 1830, William Dewees wrote from Texas to his Kentucky friend, "It would amuse you very much could you hear the manner in which the people of this new country address each other. It is nothing uncommon for us to inquire of a man why he ran away from the States! but few persons feel insulted by such a question. They generally answer for some crime or other which they have committed; if they deny having committed any crime, and say they did not run away, they are generally looked upon rather suspiciously."[85]

Bettie kept her eyes open and her horse-drawn wagon moving ever forward over the rutted forest path. Thirty miles to the northeast, after at least a day's ride, looking behind

---

her on the road and scanning hillsides and forest for Indians, she came to the Navasota River, a tributary of the Brazos then known as the Navasot, at a crossing near Old Macy. The river was flooding, and there were no ferries or bridges. It had been a historic year for flooding in the Brazos watershed: Heavy rains had fallen since April, and both the Colorado and Brazos were flooding. *Creighton's History of Brazoria County* recounts: "Day after day, great trees and islands of drift swirled down the quickening reddish waters of the Brazos. As the river neared bank level, creeks filled with backwater and crept slowly and silently onward, covering the whole country in one vast sheet of water. ... Planters built rafts and loaded their families, slaves, and goods on board to wait the recession of the flood. ... Farther down the river, it still rose slowly until its crest moved out to sea. ... Behind was left a thick layer of silt, which emitted a sourish stench. Mosquitoes bred by the millions." By June 23, the largest flood had passed, but it left behind a cholera epidemic, scourging "the whole lower Brazos country."[86]

Several families also bound for Nacogdoches were encamped on the west bank of the Navasota, waiting for the river to subside, but it was still on the rise. Bettie had crossed a lot of rivers in her thirty-five years. The river surging before her and the children now was terrifying, but what was thought to be closing in behind them was even more so. Seeing her intention, the other settlers implored her not to try to ford the river, but she shouted to them, "If we remain here, we shall be killed by the Indians![87] I would rather drown than see my children tomahawked!"[88]

She tied the wagon to a tree, unhitched one horse, and fitted it with the sidesaddle she had had the presence of mind to load into the wagon. She then put the oldest child

---

[86] Mona M. Fenn, "The Complete Story,"
http://lifeonthebrazosriver.com/MonaMFenn.htm.
[87] Melvin "Getting in Touch with Texas Roots," *Dallas Morning News*.
[88] Murray, "Home Life on Early Ranches of Southwest Texas."

behind her, handing him a bag of gold brought from Ireland that embodied their entire savings. She wrapped Baby Elizabeth in a shawl, and, holding her in her arms, spurred the horse into the flooding river.

Here, just for a moment, we have to imagine that her thoughts flitted to an alternate reality, one in which she saw herself and Robert coming in from a stable to a small but comfortable stone cottage in a pasture in northern Ireland, warming their hands near the fireplace while Kitty, Hugh, and the other children ran and played safely around the house. There was warm bread on a wooden table spread with the finest linen from her father's factory. On her shelf were books from her childhood mixed with new books from her most recent trip into Derry. Friends were coming over for supper. What would have been so wrong with that, she must have now asked herself.

The water raged, but the horse swam and eventually clambered onto the east bank. There she met some more refugees who also had been warned. She entrusted the swaddled baby to her oldest. She then swam back across the river alone, we imagine having kicked off her shoes and with her long cotton skirt billowing downstream in the churning brown water. Tying a large bundle of their things on the back of the pack horse, she took the two remaining children on the second pony with her, one in front, the other behind, and, leading the pack horse, she crossed again. Halfway across the river, Bettie heard her oldest daughter, who was watching the pony with the pack behind Bettie, cry out, "Oh, Ma! Your coat's in the water gettin' wet!"[89]

On reaching the east bank she rearranged the packs, including the bag of gold, and adjusted them on the pack horse, fixing a place where the two older children could ride.

---

[89] A.W. Buchanan writes in 1932 (*Bryan Daily Eagle*) that when Bettie would tell the story, "This incident of the child telling her that her coat was getting wet seemed to please the old lady more than any other incident of the whole trip, when she would tell it after she had become a very old lady."

The many varying accounts of this episode present some confusion with regard to just who was with her on the day of the Navasota crossing: If it was indeed in October 1833, she would have had not two children, as several accounts say, and not four, as most say, and not five as another says, but *seven* living children: Hugh, 12; John, 11; Katherine, 5; James, 4; Margaret, 2; Stafford, 1; and Elizabeth, 11 weeks. Either the date is wrong, the headcount is off, or there is some lost explanation of why her other three children were not with her. Perhaps some of the older children had been taken on to Nacogdoches by a relative or other Staggers Point neighbor. Perhaps the older boys, 12 and 11, had gone with Robert as junior minutemen, a strange detail to be left out of any account but a distinct possibility; a twelve-year-old boy on the frontier with a Kentucky rifle would have been a deadly military asset. But whether there were two, four, five, or seven, what is certain is that she thrice crossed the flooding Navasota — twice on horseback and once swimming — and however many children were with her made it across alive.

Fastening several smaller packs and bundles to the horse she was riding, she started out on a journey of four or five days and nights along the rough road, eating only dried bison, nursing a three-month-old baby, camping in the shadows and out-of-sight ravines when too tired to go on. She saw other travelers on the road, but not another settlement. Clinging to their ponies, they forded the Trinity, the Neches, and the Angelina, along with all the innumerable creeks that feed them.

In a state of fatigue we can only faintly imagine, they at last reached the fort at Nacogdoches. Soon, she learned that those who had remained on the west bank of the Navasota, "every man, woman, and child," had been butchered.[90]

At the fort, Bettie planted a garden and did a little farming to help them get by. According to family tradition,

[90] Melvin, "Getting in Touch with Texas Roots," *Dallas Morning News*.

Robert remained gone, chasing Indians, for two full years, from October 1833 to October of 1835. But where did he go, how many did he chase, and with whom? Our one and only clue is a lone sentence that reports he joined a company of Indian fighters led by "Capt. Reed."[91]

Two years of continuous riding and fighting would be an extraordinary feat for anyone, let alone a farmer. We're told that during these two years (and an additional year encompassing the Texas Revolution), Bettie never once saw her husband and heard from him very seldom. But the records show a daughter, Ann, born in 1835, so perhaps there was at least one visit.

On November 13, three weeks after Bettie and the children arrived in Nacogdoches, the earth crossed the debris stream of the Tempel-Tuttle comet, whose elliptical orbit takes it around the sun every thirty-three years. If she and the children had been outside (and they were never inside for very long) they would have witnessed, under the dark skies of colonial Nacogdoches, the greatest astronomical spectacle in recorded history. It would become known as "the night the stars fell." Across North America, people of every background stared in wonder at the night sky as ten thousand meteors per hour blazed toward earth. Some observers, quite reasonably, assumed that the world was coming to an end, and went into hysterics. This reaction was sometimes fueled

[91] Nell J. Atkins, Daughters of Republic of Texas, Patriot Ancestor Album, Volume 1, p. 132. There are three plausible candidates for whom this "Captain Reed" might have been but no strong frontrunners. The only Reed in the area who definitely became a captain was Capt. Henry Reed. He arrived in Robertson County in January 1835, and so would have had to begin fighting immediately for Robert to have served any significant time under him, but there is no mention in his biographies of Indian fighting, only service against Mexico. Wilson Reed was a close neighbor and did fight in 1839's Battle of Horn Hill, but he is nowhere referred to as a captain that we can find. Jacob Reed arrived in nearby Burleson County May 9, 1831, and, interestingly, was awarded his land grant on the Yegua River. (McLean, Papers, Vol. 6, p. 235) Perhaps the fact that the Indian attack allegedly occurred on the Yegua suggests a connection to Jacob Reed, but there is little other information to go on. Additionally, the name could be misspelled and actually be "Reid" or "Redd," which would open up many other candidates.

by widespread religious millennialism. Others were better able to appreciate nature's fireworks for what they were.

Back at Staggers Point, Mary Fullerton Henry, the wife of Robert's brother William, was in labor in their little cabin on Peach Creek.[92] She must have thought that the spectacular show in the night sky outside her glassless cabin window was simply the result of her pain. She was giving birth to William Jr., who would be known as "Bud," and, by some accounts, was the first white child born in what would become Robertson County.[93] Bud was born on a one-legged bed built into the corner of their mud-daubed hut.

---

[92] *The Hearne Democrat,* August 30, 1936.

[93] This oft-repeated "first white child" distinction for William Henry Jr. in 1835 would seem at odds with the fact that Bettie had borne Peggy (Margaret) in 1830, Stafford in 1832, and Elizabeth in 1833, all presumably at Staggers Point, within modern Robertson County.

6.

New Arrivals

IN 1835, WHILE ROBERT WAS CHASING Indians and Bettie and the children were holed up in Nacogdoches, an ox-drawn wagon train arrived at the little capital of the Robertson Colony, Sarahville de Viesca. Two families were in the caravan just entering the area, just as the Henrys had, from Greene County, Alabama. One was the family of James Head, who in just a few years would be serving in the Texas Congress. The other was that of James' best friend and his wife's brother, Elias "Eli" Seale.[94]

It's not clear when the Henrys and the Seales first met, but in the coming years the families would join together like a zipper. In time, three Henry children would marry Seales: two daughters would marry two of the Seales' sons, and one Henry son would marry the daughter of one of Eli's three brothers. (Eli's brothers followed him to fight in the Texas Revolution but later returned to the Deep South.) Even grandchildren in each family would end up marrying. This multi-generational pair-bonding was common on the frontier,

---

[94] Jim Boyd, *Grandfather's Journal: The Record of the First Seale Family in Texas,* (Indiatlantic, Fla.: Self-published, 2003), p 22.

where large families found themselves together in relative isolation. At least it made for compact family reunions.

Eli and his wife, Susannah, both had been born in North Carolina and had gradually moved west through Georgia, Alabama, and Mississippi through a long, complicated series of moves in which grown siblings followed their parents, aunts and uncles, and each other to various rural destinations where the grass was always presumed to be greener. As a nineteen-year-old in a Mississippi militia, Eli had served as a fifer in the War of 1812.[95] By 1835, Eli and his best friend and brother-in-law, James Head, were ready to make their final push into the promised land.

James Alfred Head (1797-1872) and Eli Seale (1793-1857)

Now forty-two, Eli received his land claim in Robertson's Colony well north of Staggers Point in modern Limestone County, but because of the Indian threat, he opted to settle

---

[95] Boyd, *Grandfather's Journal*, p. 8.

downstream, in what would become Brazos County.

Before he could even get settled, Eli had enlisted in a type of militia formed just that year, not by the Mexican government but by the Stephen F. Austin-created General Council of Texas, in other words, by settlers for their own defense. They were called the Texas Rangers because, like the Indians they were formed to pursue, they would need to leave behind home and hearth and range over large distances.

The Rangers were formed by an act that was passed October 17, 1835, by the General Council. Silas Parker became superintendent of the very first unit and appointed Eli Hillhouse as its captain on October 23 at Fort Sterling, which would become known in later years as Fort Parker. Though the men were scheduled to report to the Waco village to become properly organized, there was no time. The company of seven men left that day to pursue Indians in the area, most likely the Indians who had attacked the home of the McLennan family in Williamson County earlier that month. Three days later, Capt. Hillhouse sent Ranger Joseph Parker, Silas' older brother, back to get more guns, ammunition, and men.

One of the men he found that day was Eli Seale, who was recruited into the unit, making him among the first eleven Texas Rangers in history. Each unit formed during this period was responsible for ranging along the line of settlement between the major rivers. Eli's unit of about twenty-five men was responsible for ranging along the line of settlement between the Brazos and the Trinity rivers. Silas reported on November 2 from Fort Sterling, "I have used my utmost exertion to raise the company and a large majority of the company is now in the woods pursuant to my order. I took the responsibility on myself to instruct the officer to pursue a fresh Indian trail that had been made by late depredators."[96]

---

[96] Silas Parker to Council of November 2, 1835 in Jenkins, *Papers*, II: 303.

Silas Parker, like Eli, also had claimed land in Limestone County but unlike Eli had decided to settle there. Parker too had children at home, the youngest named Cynthia Ann. The very next year, Silas Parker was killed defending his home, and Cynthia Ann was carried on horseback full-speed to the northwest to spend nearly the rest of her life as a Comanche.

Eli served for just over three months — the standard tour of duty — with his unit of twenty-five Rangers and a Cherokee scout named Catfish.

Though school children might imagine that every Texan arose in unison to sacrificially free Texas from both its Mexican tyranny and indigenous terror, a December 17 report from Silas Parker to the General Council at San Felipe paints a different picture:

> Through much difficulty, I have engaged about thirty of the rangers under my superintendence. Several of them have lost their horses and the horses continue dying, so that it is extremely difficulty to keep horses for them. I find it very difficult to procure provisions. Indeed, I cannot engage any beef or pork for them though store is plenty in the country. Such is the indifference of the people as to the cause of Texas. I have no other chance but to go to those that has cattle to spare and have them valued myself; and the people of my vicinity has turned out all the beef that we had... The Indians has committed no depredations since my last. The boys are zealously engaged and I hope their labors will be of the most vital importance to those fe[ar]less adventurers that has reclaimed this fertile country from savage haunts.[97]

---

[97] Jenkins, *Papers*, III: 230.

But though it was a short stint, he earned the respect of his fellow Rangers. On Christmas Eve, while Silas Parker was away at San Felipe de Austin, the company's captain, Eli Hillhouse, was killed in an Indian fight. Without a commander, the unit held an election, and Eli Seale was made captain. When Parker returned and met the Rangers at Viesca, also known as "The Falls on the Brazos," he made the promotion official.[98]

One should not picture Eli the Texas Ranger with a pressed gray uniform and felt Stetson. The Rangers at this point were the very definition of a rag-tag paramilitary. He probably wore buckskin, a wide-brimmed hat to keep off the sun and rain, and packed two pistols, a rifle (in a horse holster), and a Bowie knife. And though our only photo of Eli shows him clean shaven, probably on his wedding day, he would have been grizzled by long weeks in the field without a mirror or any of the hygienic advantages of home, meager as even those were. It was said that all the typical early Ranger had was a saddle (which doubled as his pillow), a canteen, and a Mexican blanket.[99]

We also know their daily rations: three-quarters of a pound of salt pork or bacon *or* one and a quarter pounds of fresh or salted beef; a pound and a half of bread, hardtack (elsewhere known as sea biscuit), flour, or cornmeal; peas or beans; and rice, coffee, vinegar, salt, and sugar — all of which fluctuated based on shortages and surpluses. Occasionally soap and candles were thrown in.[100] But they might also have gone into the field with nothing but a canteen and a pouch of cold flour. Cold flour was the Southern name for parched corn meal, a trail food that had existed among the American Indians since before contact. In the East, it was known as rockahominy. The Spanish called it *pinole*. "Cold flour" was a corruption of "coal flour," from

---

[98] Boyd, *Grandfather's Journal*,

[99] Gwynn, *Empire of the Summer Moon*.

[100] Boyd, *Grandfather's Journal*.

the coals the corn was roasted in before being ground to a fine, space-saving powder.[101] A little sugar in the mix helped it go down. All of this would have been supplemented by any game they could shoot along the way.

If you had ridden into the Claypan in the late thirties or forties and had wanted to speak to Eli, you would have asked for "Major Seale." He was never officially promoted to major but it was the honorific he would answer to for the rest of his days. It should be added that he was more of a "major" than Elvis' Tom Parker or fried chicken's Harland Sanders were "colonels"; the nickname was drawn from the respect he commanded from the community as a leader and from his role as a de facto leader in a number of Indian engagements during a later Ranger stint. [102]

By January 25, 1836, Eli and his men had fulfilled their obligation and were discharged back to civilian life. Eli rode to Columbus to register the muster rolls of his men and collect his pay, a quest that would drag on for years. The main problem was that the polity he was trying to collect from was in utter turmoil.[103]

In 1838, Eli learned that the Rangers who had served under him three years earlier still had not received their pay. He might have been patriotic, but that did not mean he served solely out of the goodness of his heart. He was adamant that he and his men be paid and wrote to the Texas Senate and House of Representatives. In the one-page letter he explained that when General Houston was retreating from west to east before the Mexican Army, he had ordered San Felipe de Austin to be burned, and that the records of Eli's men's service had thus been destroyed. He requested the Senate and House "provide some measures by which these men might obtain their just and legally acquired rights." Both chambers appointed a committee to evaluate

---

[101] Horace Kephart, *Camping and Woodcraft*, 1910.

[102] Boyd, *Grandfather's Journal,*

[103] Boyd, *Grandfather's Journal,*

the petition. The joint committee, not grasping Eli's explanation or not understanding the effects of fire on paper, reported out unfavorably because there were "no accompanying records." Eventually, with the aid of the muster roll Eli had submitted, the Texas Congress relented, and all Eli's men, including Catfish the Cherokee scout, had their payday.[104]

Throughout the 1830s, despite all the chaos of two wars, settlers continued to stream into the area. At Staggers Point, as more Henry brothers arrived and their wives kept having children, the families' penchant for using the same set of names generation after generation became more problematic. (At least it makes research more challenging.) The natural fix for living with this paucity of appellations was the adoption of nicknames, which everyone seem to be assigned. Bettie was "Aunt Bettie" to the whole community, and later "Grandma Henry." The "Aunt This," and "Uncle That" convention was extremely popular, whether there was any blood relation or not, and in retrospect rendered community life somehow more homey. Robert became widely known as "Squire Henry."

Eli, a product of the eighteenth century South, had siblings with entertaining names like Littleton and Bluford, Sethright and Moses, and Jilson and Temperance. He opted to name his own sons for the heroes of his day, but here too nicknames prevailed over given names. Eli's oldest son, Christopher Columbus Seale, became simply "Clum," and Clum's baby brother, Bradford (undoubtedly after Gov. William Bradford of the Mayflower colony) became "Bird" and "Uncle Brad," but was usually simply "B.T. Seale" on documents. Brad's children, in turn, would be named for heroes of a new era: George Washington Seale, Sam Houston Seale, Robert Lee Seale, and so on.

And if your name happened to be James and you lived at Staggers Point, you were better known by one of the

---

[104] Boyd, *Grandfather's Journal*, p. 49.

following politically incorrect monikers: Deaf Jim, One-eyed Jim, Flop-eared Jim, Whiskey Jim, Whispering Jim, or Dutch Jim.[105] Nearby lived Clubfoot Johnson, and a little later, One-Armed Chatham. Nothing worked to resolve ambiguity like taking a person's most noticeable handicap and making it the centerpiece of their identity.

---

[105] *Brazos County History.*

Transcript:

Houston May 28, 1838

To the Hon. Senate and House of Representatives of the Republic of Texas in Congress assembled. Your petitioner in behalf of himself & the company under his command beg (illegible) respectfully to represent to your honourable body that in the Fall of the year 1835 I had a company of men under my command who were authorized to be raised by the provisional government of the Consultation at San Felipe De Austin for its protection and defence of the Frontier — That they served faithfully and received honourable discharge from under my hand, which discharges were deposited in the general land office then at San Felipe for the purpose of being audited. A part of these discharges was destroyed at the destruction of that place by command of General Houston at the approach of the Mexican Army. Consequently the petitions of the same could not be made to the General Land Office at Houston. By this means those men have been deprived of their just rights and legal property.

It is therefore respectfully requested by your memorialist that your honourable body will take some action upon this subject and provide some measures by which these men may obtain their just and legally acquired rights and your petitioner will ever pray to—

Eli Seale

7.

Blood on the Hyacinth: Revolution

ON MARCH 6, 1836, six weeks after Eli had returned to his nascent farm in upper Robertson County, and just as Robert was thinking of returning to Nacogdoches to retrieve Betty and the children, a former Spanish mission in San Antonio that had been occupied by Texians fell to General Santa Anna's thousands. When word of the fall of the Alamo reached Eli, he re-enlisted, this time not as a Ranger but as regular army. But first, he and James Head sent their families out of Texas, escorted by Eli's brothers who had followed him to Texas spoiling for a military adventure. Thus these families joined what became known to history as the Runaway Scrape, a terrible civilian exodus east out of Texas fleeing before the Mexican advance. The Texas Rangers provided rear guard for this civilian retreat, helping sick and starving settler families ford streams and rivers, and all the while trying to keep Indians at bay.[106]

---

[106] Boyd, *Grandfather's Journal*,

William Dewees wrote:

> Every manner of crossing rivers was resorted
> to at this time; there being but few ferries and
> the water-courses very high. We were
> frequently obliged to tax our inventive
> faculties to find methods for crossing. To give
> you an example of our difficulties, I will tell
> you the manner in which we crossed the San
> Jacinto river. There were about seventy-five
> wagons in the company, and on arriving at the
> river we found no way to cross; the river was
> up to the top of the banks, and there was no
> ferry; the question arose how are we to get
> across! we might construct rafts but the
> stream was so rapid that it would be
> hazardous to cross on them! yet cross we
> must, and some way must be thought of. But
> thanks to the invention of two Yankees, the
> difficulty was soon obviated. They proposed
> that we should look us out a couple of very tall
> pine trees, so that their length might be
> sufficient to reach across the river, cut them
> down, peel the bark from them and then lay
> them across the river so near to each other
> that we might place the wagons on them and
> pull them across the river with a rope. This we
> did, upon each loaded wagon we placed a
> number of women and children, and the
> seventy-five wagons were all drawn over in
> the course of half a day.[107]

On March 9, three days after the fall of the Alamo,
Robert Henry enlisted as well.[108] Bettie and the children

---

[107] Dewees, *Letters from an Early Settler of Texas*, p. 204.

[108] Historical marker at Robert Henry grave gives period of service as
beginning on March 9.

would have to stay hunkered in Nacogdoches still longer.[109] The path of Robert's service is at times murky, but there is some evidence that he was a trusted messenger among high-level officials, and though it involves some conjecture, we can piece together an educated guess as to where he went and what he was doing.

On April 7, 1836, Major R.M. Williamson (Three-legged Willie) wrote to Sam Houston:

Washington, [on the Brazos]

April 7th, 1836

To General Houston,

Since writing this morning by Major [Robert] Barr, I realized that I omitted stating to you that one of our spies, Daniel Gray, returned last night. He gives information of a chase given him by a party of mounted men, in number eight, supposed by him to be Mexicans. I think he is mistaken. Five men are still out in the same direction and well mounted and have had time to report. I take them to be a party of your spies that have given chase. In a few hours we will know the truth.

Yours ably,

R M Williamson, Maj.

P.S. Write me [immediately] upon receipt of this. A Mr. Henry told me you wished me to come down [to see] you. I have no acquaintance with this Henry and think you would have written me to that effect if

---

[109] Burkhart, "Pioneer Ancestors"

[imploring?].

Williamson[110]

Although there were two Mr. Henrys in Houston's service at this time, we know that Houston used Robert as a messenger on a later occasion, of which more later. And so it is likely that this is Robert. By knowing Houston's whereabouts, we can know something of Robert's likely whereabouts as well.

Though Robert and General Houston had not met before, their families had apparently been friends in Ireland.[111] Houston's grandmother had lived in the same County Antrim as the Henrys before immigrating to New York, so when they did meet, they had much to discuss. As Robert joined Gillespie's command within Houston's army and moved east toward the mouth of the San Jacinto, another pivotal drama was playing out to the southwest.

The army of thirty-two-year-old Colonel James Fannin had been out-maneuvered at a little outpost near La Bahia, on the coastal plains southeast of San Antonio. Fannin and his approximately four hundred men surrendered under the pretense that they would be afforded the rights of prisoners of war and eventually paroled. On Palm Sunday, March 27, 1836, Col. Portilla marched three hundred Texians out of the fort into three columns between two rows of Mexican soldiers. Most believed they were simply being transferred elsewhere. The Texians were shot point-blank, with any survivors clubbed and stabbed to death. The forty Texians who had been unable to walk were still inside. Thirty-nine were killed inside the mission. The last, Col. Fannin, having watched all his men be executed, knew his time had come. Unable to stand, he was carried to the courtyard in front of the chapel and blindfolded in his chair. Assuming some

---

[110] http://sonsoftherepuiblicoftexas.blogspot.com/2010_03_01_archive.html
[111] Murray, "Home Life on Early Ranches of Southwest Texas."

gentlemanly ethic of war might still be in play — an assumption he should have long since abandoned — he made three requests: that his personal possessions to be sent to his family, that he be shot in the heart and not the face, and that he be given a Christian burial. The soldiers promptly took Jim Fannin's belongings, shot him in the face, and burned his body, along with all the others who had died that day.

This was the formative event of the revolution and so of all of Texas history. The Texians, who already burned for revenge for the no-quarter order given at the Alamo just three weeks earlier, were now incensed and furious and thirsty for revenge at a scale never seen before or since. We see the pattern throughout history: If the Mexican Army had just kept Fannin's men as prisoners of war and treated them with a modicum of human dignity, would the last of those Anglo farmers have come off their farms and hastened with long rifles and Bowie knives to the prairies of San Jacinto? And if they would have, would they have fought as they did? But victory wasn't enough for the Mexicans; they annihilated their enemy, and in so doing, sealed their own fate.

It is often overlooked that the martyrs of the Alamo and Goliad became such because they ignored Sam Houston's orders to destroy their outposts and retreat toward Houston's position, where they might have resupplied and lived to fight another day.[112] But every people need their shrines.

Sometime within the next few days, Robert was under Houston's direct command as a private in Capt. James Gillespie's second regiment, sixth infantry. From Gonzalez, Houston marched east for the mouth of the San Jacinto River to engage the Napoleon of the West, he who had given the no-quarter orders for both the Alamo and Goliad. As an Irishman, Robert would have had a lot of company. Some one hundred men, or one-seventh of the Texian army at San Jacinto, were Irish-born. Robert's brother William was

---

[112] Sam Houston, *The Writings of Sam Houston*, Ed. Amelia W. Williams and Eugene C. Barker (Austin: University of Texas Press, 1941).

among them.[113]

Houston's men camped seventeen times between from Gonzales and the San Jacinto. The final days and nights before arriving at the battleground illustrate the hardship and must have made Eli, Robert, and William wistful for the life a militiaman and a Ranger. Sam Houston tells the story himself:

> The main army, amounting to between seven and eight hundred men, was put in motion and marched that day (April 16), a fatiguing march of eighteen miles through the prairie.
>
> Excessive rains had made the prairie boggy and in many places the wagons had to be unloaded and the dismounted field-pieces carried or rolled through the mire.
>
> I had early in the march foreseen what lay before the men, and on the first emergency, stripped off my coat, dismounted, and set the example of unloading and transporting baggage and guns. The brave little army halted at sunset, and laid themselves down to sleep in the open field without covering for there was not a tent in the camp. About dark, a cold rain set in and continued for twenty-four hours.
>
> The next day (17th) the army pursued its exhausting march through the rain for twelve miles. Another night followed — the soldiers slept on the wet ground with their arms in their hands ready to answer in a single moment the three taps of the drum which was never touched by anyone but myself.

---

[113] Henry, "The Henry Family," *Brazos County History*, p. 227.

The third day's march (18th) through the
prairie of eighteen miles brought the army to
Post Oak Bayou, where we encamped for the
night. The toilsome march through the prairie
was now over, and we were only six or eight
miles from Harrisburg. But Santa Anna had
been there before us and reduced the town to
ashes.[114]

The chess pieces were in place. The rifles were cleaned
and loaded. But Houston had other plans for Robert. The day
before the battle, Houston gave Robert a special mission. He
told him confidentially to start off with his horse as if he
were taking it to water, but then to ride on to Dunn's Fort —
just east of Robert's home. "I am going to fight Santa Anna
tomorrow," Houston said. "You tell the folks up there I am
going to whip him, or I won't let him whip me. If they hear
the cannon, they will know the battle is on."[115] The meaning
of this last sentence is not crystal clear. Dunn's Fort was
some one hundred thirty miles to the northwest; they
wouldn't have heard cannon unless the Texians we're
retreating in a big way, hence "the battle is on." But it was
also one hundred thirty miles in the wrong direction. Any
Texian retreat would have been to the northeast or due east,
the shortest distance across the Sabine and into the
muscular embrace of Uncle Sam. And one presumes that any
Mexican retreat would simply follow the coast west then
south toward the Nueces.

There at the battle, under the command of Colonel
Edward Burleson, stood the future father-in-law of two of his
daughters. A muster roll compiled the day after battle by
Colonel Edward Burleson's clerk lists Eli Seale as one of his

---

[114] *The Autobiograph of Sam Houston*, Ed. by Donald Day and Harry Herbert
Ullom (Norman: University of Oklahoma Press, 1954) p. 116, quoted from
Yoakum, *History of Texas, II,* Writings, I, p. 410-411.
[115] Murray, "Home Life on Early Ranches of Southwest Texas."

privates.[116] The best account of what Eli must have seen and done comes to us from Creed Taylor, a settler in the DeWitt Colony, who relayed his experiences at San Jacinto.[117]

The eve of the battle was restless for "the boys," as they called each other. But the general, ever assured, slept soundly. When April 21 dawned, Houston rose from his pallet and walked to the bay to wash his face. Just then, a raven flew from the direction of the Mexican camp, something Houston, whose Cherokee-given name was The Raven, took as a good omen. The day was bright and crisp. Taylor remembers:

> From their crude pallets the boys sprang up as if for a joyous holiday. Merry jests went the rounds, and the camp wits spared neither high private nor officers. "If you get bumped off, Bill, won't you will me your coonskin cap?" Tomlinson said to a comrade: "You can take the cap now; I'll wear a Mexican officer's hat on parade tomorrow," rejoined the confident comrade.

---

[116] (BATTLE OF SAN JACINTO - April 20 & 21, 1836; from copy of list of Burleson's Command made Apr 22, 1836 by Wm. Gorham, Clerk, http://www.forttumbleweed.net/historyarmy.html)

[117] Creed Taylor as related to James T. DeShields in *Tall Men With Long Rifles*, 1935.

Col. Edward Burleson (1798-1851)
He would go on to become vice president of Texas.

But as the morning wore on, the hilarity gave way to anxiety and impatience. They had expected to attack early, and yet the delay dragged on and on. Noon came and still no forward movement. But observant soldiers did see officers approach Houston, reclining under a tree, just after noon and saw them gesturing excitedly. "I saw Houston rise up and with vehement motions of his clenched fists, address the party," remembers Taylor.

Soon, Deaf Smith, the famous scout, rode up to Houston and then, after a short exchange, spurred his horse away at a full gallop. Everyone knew that the chess pieces had been set in motion.

The men gathered around Houston and the general mounted his horse to make a speech. He told them that Vince's Bridge was at that moment being destroyed, and therefore the enemy was hemmed in. The Mexicans could not escape or receive reinforcements. By the same token neither could the Texians. It was win or die.

Remember my boys, you are fighting for Texas
and your loved ones, to avenge the inhuman
butchery of your friends and comrades at the
Alamo and at Goliad! The spirits of these
brave men call to us for revenge. Remember
your wives and little children who are now in
flight to escape the fury of the ruthless
invaders; the redbanded war lord, Santa
Anna, having boasted he would pursue and
annihilate the rebel Texans and then wash his
hands of their blood in the Sabine. The time
and the situation is here and we will win if
everyone does his duty. We must win or die.
Let us fight fast and hard.

Houston rode among the men with his sword pointing at
the Mexican camp. Taylor recalls,

Going into battle of course carries serious
feelings for most men; but I know I was not
scared. I thought only of fighting, and I
believe every man was anxious for the fray.
Somehow I felt that we would win. When our
line was formed and just before the order to
advance was given, I looked up and down the
ranks to see if anyone looked scared. The boys
had remarked about the nervous state of mind
of some of the officers and some believed them
unduly excited. As I looked into the faces of
these men I could see no signs of uneasiness.
On the contrary, there was a spirit of
cheerfulness, and levity that was remarkable
under such conditions. Captain Karnes sat
during the few minutes we remained in line
on his horse directly in front of us and replied
in his own dry, droll way to the jests of his

men in the ranks.

The company leaders barked, "Arm and line!" Bearded and ragged from forty days in the field, only one company, Captain William Wood's "Kentucky Rifles," wore uniforms. The rest sported homespun and leather. Each company formed up and was addressed by its captain. Mosley Baker "harangued" his men in such a loud voice that Houston, who was riding up and down the lines, halted and sat quietly, listening approvingly. Baker told his men neither to ask for nor to give quarter — that now was the chance to settle scores and avenge their friends at San Antonio and Goliad. As a reminder, he proposed the company carry a red flag, ad a large red handkerchief would be carried into battle on a pole.

Eli waited amid Burleson's troops, which stood rank and file two deep. He watched as Burleson, mounted on a large bay, rode up and down the line addressing his men. But they did not need his encouragement. Eager to attack they swayed forward, breaking out of line at any point an officer was not holding them back with the flat of his sword. Burleson galloped over to Sherman's line, then dashed back across the clearing, his blue flannel shirt fluttering in the breeze and sword glinting in the sun. The sight that elicited a cheer from his men.

In his muddy, quasi-military getup, Houston rode his gray horse up and down the line. *"Now hold your fire, men, until you get the order!"* Houston reined his horse to the men, drew his sword and pointed toward the Mexican encampment. *"Forward, my brave men! Charge the enemy and give them hell."* At the command, *"Advance!"* nine hundred ten settlers[118] moved quickly out of the woods and

---

[118] Quoting from James T. DeShields in *Tall Men With Long Rifles* (1935) "In his official report of the battle, April 25, 1836, Houston said 783 Texans took part. Yet in a roster published later he listed 845 officers and men at San Jacinto, and by oversight omitted Captain Alfred H. Wyly's Company. In a

up the rise. Standing together they would have easily fit within a modern football field. Burleson's regiment was in the center; Sherman's was on the left wing; the artillery, under George W. Hockley, was on Burleson's right; the infantry, under Henry Millard, was to the right of the artillery; and the cavalry, led by Lamar, was on the far right.

They began at a trot.

A fifer played the popular tune "Will You Come to the Bower I Have Shaded for You," with a battered drum playing along.[119] The love song was a ruse, meant to lull whatever Mexican soldiers might have been listening into even greater complacency if that were possible. Eli had been a fifer in the War of 1812, but with the combat experience he had accrued in the interim, it's more likely he gripped a rifle now than his old fife.

The soldiers topped a rise in the ground that had partially obscured each army from the other, and for the first time the Texians got a full look at the brush and dirt that formed the Mexican breastworks. Now the fifer changed abruptly to "Yankee Doodle," and the soldiers' trot accelerated into a full run.

Deaf Smith, who had been dispatched by Houston earlier for a then-unknown reason, came riding up, muddy, his horse foaming from the sprint. Coming up along the lines of charging foot soldiers and frantically waving an ax above overhead, he shouted, *"Vince's Bridge is gone! No escape, boys! Fight fast and hard!"* Then he wheeled toward the Mexican camp, galloped at full speed and leapt the Mexican

---

Senate speech February 28, 1859, Houston said his effective force never exceeded 700 at any point. Conclusive evidence in official records brings the total number at San Jacinto up to 910."

[119] Taylor adds "except for the time when General Havelock marched to the relief of Lucknow to the music of 'Annie Laurie' this was, so far as I know, the only time in history troops were led into battle to the strains of a love song."

barricade. His exhausted horse stumbled and fell, throwing Smith into the Mexicans' midst. Smith rose, drew his pistol, and aiming at a Mexican who was about to run him through with a bayonet, pulled the trigger. Nothing. He hurled the gun at his attacker, hitting him in the head and stunning him. As the Mexican stumbled backward, Smith seized the soldier's bayonet and killed him. This was the first blood shed on the hyacinth, the first fatality of San Jacinto.

"Like a cyclone crashing through the forest, we went over the dirt and brush barricade without halting," Taylor remembers. "A solid sheet of flame flashed from our rifles, and then, without waiting to reload, we bore down and closed in upon the surprised and frightened enemy with clubbed guns, pistols, and hunting knives. It was a hand-to-hand struggle; and now came the cry, *"Remember the Alamo! Remember Goliad!"*

The battle famously lasted just eighteen minutes, a fact that tells one everything he needs to know about the conflict: in fact, it was not a battle at all, but an ambush carried out in broad daylight with fife and drum. And it was won almost as soon as it started. The fact that Santa Anna had not even posted lookouts speaks to the incredible hubris of the dictator-general. The Mexican battle plan was to rest up until they were good and ready, and then kill the hapless rebels, who after all were trapped against water. It apparently never occurred to them that the Texians might actually go on offense.

Whatever moral superiority the Texians might have maintained over the Mexicans heretofore because of the no-quarter massacres at the Alamo and Goliad now began quickly to evaporate. The Mexicans were beaten. Houston shouted to his men to stand down, but it was no use. They were possessed by revenge and in a berserker's rage, as if channeling their bearded and dirty Viking ancestors of a thousand years before. They mercilessly butchered the Mexican soldiers, who now threw down their guns and cried,

"Me no Alamo!" "Me no Goliad!" to no avail. The crazed settlers reloaded and chased after the stampeding Mexicans, shooting, stabbing, clubbing them to death. Taylor remembers that "from the moment of the first collision the battle was a slaughter, frightful to behold. The fugitives ran in wild terror over the prairie and into the boggy marshes, but the avengers of the Alamo and Goliad followed and slew them, or drove them into the waters to drown. Men and horses, dead and dying, in the morass in the rear and right of the Mexican camp, formed a bridge for the pursuing Texans. Blood reddened the water. General Houston tried to check the execution but the fury of his men was beyond restraint."

The Mexican cavalrymen who tried to escape over Vince's Bridge soon learned the truth. In desperation, some horsemen spurred their horses down the steep bank; some dismounted and plunged into the swollen stream. "The Texians poured a deadly fire into Mexicans struggling in the flood."[120]

"No me mates" (don't kill me) was heard on every hand, but the Texians continued the butchery with their Bowie knives, using their own emptied guns as clubs, and stabbing Mexicans with their own bayonets. Houston remembered later that the battle was eighteen minutes but that the killing went on for an hour. Ruthless and grotesque as it was, it should be remembered that unlike the Mexicans at San Antonio and Goliad, the Texians finally did begin to take prisoners, and that indeed, in the end their prisoners outnumbered their victims, seven hundred three to six hundred thirty. That night, the prisoners sat huddled within a huge ring of fires, and pleaded with the Texians by the only words the Texians had inadvertently taught them. One of a few Mexican women who had accompanied the Army threw herself at the feet of one of Seguin's Tejano soldiers and pleaded, "Senor God Damn, do not kill me for the love of God and the life of your mother!" Then turning to her

---

[120] L.W. Kemp and Ed Kilman, *The Battle of San Jacinto and the San Jacinto Campaign*, http://www.tamu.edu/faculty/ccbn/dewitt/batsanjacinto.htm

companions, she cried, "See here sisters! This Senor God Damn speaks the Christian language [Spanish] like the rest of us!"[121]

As HOUSTON HAD ORDERED, Robert had ridden for Dunn's Fort on the eve of the battle, a trip that would have taken three to four days, and delivered the message.

Capt. James Dunn had probably sailed from Ireland with the Henrys, along with his wife, Isabella, and a newborn baby, Mary. It is said that Isabella and Mary combined weighed ninety-six pounds (including the baby's clothes!). The reason we know this is that James paid for their passage with tobacco, pound for pound. New World fare must have agreed with Isabella, as she tipped the scales at two hundred pounds by the time of her death. James had first built his log cabin at the site of the fort. A shed room served as the kitchen; his slaves lived in the attic. He converted the site into a fort by standing long logs on end in a deep trench to form a palisade and cutting port holes between the logs. Having led a daring life his kin in Ireland could scarcely have believed, James Dunn met quite a mundane end. In August 1851, he was preparing to leave Texas and go back to Ireland in order to secure some of the Dunn estate. On the eve of his departure, he went out on the porch for his customary evening smoke. Judging that his pipe was too close for comfort to the log pillar supporting the porch, James scooted his chair forward so that he might then lean back. The chair leg went over the edge and took James with it. He injured his back and a few days later, died, age fifty-seven.[122]

Robert would have passed within a few miles of his log home on the way to and from Dunn's Fort, and he might have even dropped by the old cabin for a look, but it would

---

[121] James, Marquis, *The Raven: A Biography of Sam Houston* (University of Texas Press: Austin 1929, 1988), p. 253.
[122] McLean, *Papers*, Vol. 9, p. 238.

have been a sad sight, for Bettie and the children had been at Nacogdoches for more than two years, and nature would have been quickly taking back the old Henry place. When he returned to the mouth of the San Jacinto, the battle was over. It is not an exaggeration to claim that, though humble in scope and short in duration, next to Washington's victory at Yorktown, the Battle of San Jacinto was the most consequential military engagement in American history, not for the freedom of Texas, but for what that freedom portended. Had Santa Anna won and Texas remained part of Mexico, Texas would not have become American, and the Mexican-American War, which gave the United States territory that would become California, New Mexico, Arizona, Nevada, Utah, and parts of Wyoming and Colorado, might never have occurred.

Antonio Lopez de Santa Anna (1794-1876), in 1853

During the battle, multiple horses had been shot from underneath Houston, and the general's leg was shattered just above the ankle by a rifle ball. After Houston had secured Santa Anna's surrender, he required surgery on his leg. It was Robert's unit, led by Captain Gillespie, that escorted Houston to the *Flora*, a dirty little schooner that took him to New Orleans for surgery. It's not clear if Robert would have been back in time to join in this transfer, but whether he was or not, this is the sight that greeted him as he rode back onto the battlefield he had left days earlier:

The Mexican dead, more than six hundred thirty of them, were neither burned nor buried, but lay exactly where they had fallen — "everywhere and in every position," as Creed Taylor recalls. "It was a ghastly sight I can never forget." There were three reasons they were not buried: First, the Texians were tired, and burying more than six hundred men would require very significant effort. Second, they were busy, what with guarding the baggage at Harrisburg and watching the seven hundred three prisoners. Third, they simply didn't care, and apparently, neither did Santa Anna. "Santa Anna evinced no desire to have his slain men interred, and of course we Texans were not concerned about the final disposition of these unfortunate 'greasers,'" Taylor recalls.

On Robert's return, some men might have still been wandering the field gathering up guns and swords and other souvenirs. The boys amused themselves by dressing up their mules and horses with the Mexican officers' sashes, ribbons, and gold tinsels. The most extreme example of collecting was not provided by a soldier at all but an enterprising dentist from the States, who, hearing of the large loss of life, hastened to the battlefield to methodically go from body to body, extracting gold and silver teeth from the corpses. "No one disturbed him in his gruesome work," remembers Taylor.

Soon, drenched by the heavy April showers and then baked by the burning May sun, the bodies presented "a fearful, most ghastly sight, swelling to enormous sizes and decaying with a revolting stench. No one, of course, wanted to engage in the gruesome work. The boys saying that they came to kill, but not to bury Mexicans, and it was jocosely suggested that a dead 'greaser' would turn to a mummy anyhow — that there was not vitality enough about them to cause decomposition; that at the Alamo and at Goliad our dead were burned, but that we would be more humane and leave the unfortunate Mexicans to rest in peace on the field."

With that much carnage, one would think that the sky above would be black with Texas' ubiquitous turkey vultures. But witnesses reported that the smell was so bad, the few vultures and wolves that came around limited their diet to the fallen horses. The odor forced the Texian army to move up to Harrisburg. Taylor writes, "After the flesh rotted off, the cattle pawed over and chewed the bones to the extent that their milk and meat was unfit for use. The citizens of the vicinity then gathered up and buried the bones, all except the skulls, which could not be chewed. The skulls lay on the ground and some of them could be seen many years later. Some of them were carried away as souvenirs;" wrote Taylor, "but I never had any desire for such relics."[123]

We seldom consider that the San Jacinto battlefield was not the publicly owned nature preserve it is today but rather someone's property. The landowner, one Mrs. McCormick, was none too pleased with the mess history had left behind and paid a visit to General Houston at his headquarters requesting him to "have them stinking Mexicans removed from [my] land." Houston answered with mock grandiosity, "Madam, your land will be famed in history as the classic spot upon which the glorious victory of San Jacinto was won. Here that last scourge of mankind, the arrogant, self-styled Napoleon of the West, met his fate."

Mrs. McCormick was somewhat less sentimental about the event, and replied, "To the devil with your glorious history! Take off your stinking Mexicans!"

---

[123] Taylor, DeShields, *Tall Men with Long Rifles*,
http://www.tamu.edu/faculty/ccbn/dewitt/sanjacintotaylor.htm

April turned to May, and May to June. And it was not only the Mexican dead who had been neglected. The beginning of June found General Thomas Rusk, whom Houston had made commander in chief upon his departure for New Orleans, and his command escorting Santa Anna's second in command, Gen. Vicente Filisola, back to the new Mexican border, the border Santa Anna had agreed to, the Rio Grande. On about June 3, the Texan army reached Goliad, and Rusk took it upon himself to give the Texas dead there — whose charred bodies had been rotting in the fields and getting devoured by wolves, vultures, and coyotes — a proper military burial. Henry family tradition holds that Robert himself wrapped the charred body of Fannin in a flag and buried it.[124] At eight-thirty the next morning, Rusk orchestrated a parade, and when it reached the burial site, he delivered the eulogy himself:

> Surrounded in the open prairie by this fearful odds, cut off from provisions and even water, they were induced, under the sacred promise of receiving the treatment usual to prisoners of war, to surrender. They were marched back, and for a week treated with the utmost inhumanity and barbarity. They were marched out of yonder fort under the pretense of getting provisions, and it was not until the firing of musketry [and] the shrieks of the dying, that they were satisfied of their approaching fate. Some endeavored to make their escape, but they were pursued by the ruthless cavalry and most of them cut down with their swords... Many a tender and

---

[124] Murray, "Home Life on Early Ranches of Southwest Texas." Robert Henry's name is not found among those in Rusk's command during this escort, but if the family tradition that he buried Fannin is correct, then he would have been. The Murray account says that Robert arrived "soon after the massacre," but this timeline is impossible since Mexican soldiers occupied the site until well after the Battle of San Jacinto, fleeing south just before the arrival of Rusk's escort.

affectionate woman will remember, with tearful eye, 'La Bahia.' But we have another consolation to offer. It is, that while liberty has a habitation and a name, their chivalrous deeds will be handed down upon the bright pages of history. We can still offer another consolation: Santa Anna, the mock hero, the black-hearted murderer, is within our grasp. Yea, and there he must remain, tortured with the keen pain of corroding conscience. He must oft remember La Bahia, and while the names of those whom he murdered shall soar to the highest pinnacle of fame, his shall sink down into the lowest depths of infamy and disgrace."[125]

Filisola continued to lead the retreat of some four thousand Mexican soldiers until they crossed the Rio Grande into Matamoros, with Rusk's company following like police in a modern-day low-speed chase.

In June 1836, Robert mustered out of the army, and began the long trip to reunite with his family, wending his way north along the coastal plains and prairie and finally through the piney woods toward Nacogdoches. On arrival, he was "greatly surprised at how well they had been cared for,"[126] and he must have been both thrilled and shocked to see his children, especially Elizabeth, who had been an infant and now was a hearty three-year-old. As a Henry neighbor once put it, "the children had grown out of his knowledge."[127]

But what sort of life awaited them in this wild new republic? And did they even have a home at Staggers Point to return to?

---

[125] http://www.presidiolabahia.org/massacre.htm#2
[126] Henry, "The Henry Family," *Brazos County History*, p. 227.
[127] A.W. Buchanan, *The Bryan Daily Eagle*, October, 4, 1932.

8.

The More Things Change . . .

WHEN BETTIE AND THE CHILDREN had arrived at Nacogdoches in October 1833, they were still toting their bag of gold. But conditions were such in their little hut that she didn't trust its safety for the long haul. So she gave it to a neighbor for safekeeping. When Robert arrived in Nacogdoches to retrieve the family, the neighbor could not be found, but Robert was impatient to finally go home. "Oh, I guess he has gone with it — let's let it go and get back home where we can soon make some more," he said.

On the very same ponies that had brought them, the Henrys started the one hundred fifty-mile trip back down the Old San Antonio Road. By some means, word had come to Bettie at Nacogdoches that a settler in Macy had secured the wagon and harnesses that she had abandoned on the west bank of the Navasota. So after fording a much calmer

Navasota this time, they made the three-mile detour to Macy and found the man, who, sure enough, had kept the wagon in good shape for them and had kept the gear, "right down to the harness string." This kind act was just the first two affirmations of humanity that would come in quick succession, and of which they were in sore need.

They arrived home in time to plant a late crop that put them in good stead for the coming year. A few months, perhaps as long as a year, had passed when one day Bettie heard a crashing thud on her front porch. She came out to investigate and saw a man on horseback riding away. The stranger called back to her, "I left a package for Bettie Henry!" She looked down, and to her delight it was the bag of gold. Moreover, she did not believe the string that tied it shut had even been loosened in all the time it had been in the possession of either the neighbor or the courier. When telling the story in later years, she invariably wound it up in the same way: "Oh, my children, them was honest folks we had in them days."[128]

History books say the war ended in April, but the situation was far from settled, and Eli Seale continued serving in the Army until October. On July 16, 1836, Eli enlisted in Captain Nicholas Lynch's First Regiment Volunteers. In September 1836, he transferred into the company of Captain William D. Burnett.[129]

We also know that on September 5, Eli was at Dimitt's Landing, a privately run pier and warehouse at the mouth of the Lavaca River built to handle imports. We know he was there because he and all other members of the army there

---

[128] A.W. Buchanan, *The Bryan Daily Eagle*, October, 4, 1932. In other versions of this story, a man takes the bag of gold on the east bank of the Navasota as the family is scrambling up following their crossing but disappears in the chaos, only to find her and return the bag, unopened, in Nacogdoches months later.

[129] http://www.txgenweb.org/tx/muster.html, pp. 58 and 99.

who hailed from what was then Milam County cast their first votes in the new republic.[130] There were a lot of decisions to be made and thus a lot of votes to be cast in setting up the new republic. On the same day up in Staggers Point, Robert, William, and thirty-three others voted. A few months earlier, William and Hugh had ridden over to Tenoxtitlan to cast votes for independence and for their delegate to the convention.[131] (George Childress was elected delegate with fifty-five votes, with Sterling Clack Robertson coming a distant third with fourteen votes.) But this time, the vote was taken at William Henry's home. The settlers might have disagreed on some things, but there was virtual unanimity that day: Sam Houston won every vote for president, and Mirabeau Lamar won most of the votes for vice president. Sterling Robertson became senator that day with a commanding thirty votes. And the settlers of Staggers Point were unanimous on the two propositions: that the Texas constitution should be adopted as presented and that Texas should attach itself to the United States.[132] With all the swagger Texans have enjoyed about Texas once being its own republic, it is clear that the citizens of that republic — with the notable exception of Lamar, who harbored visions of a Republic of Texas that rivaled the United States and stretched all the way to the Pacific — wanted nothing more than to be Americans. But at least for the time being, it was unrequited love. The U.S. Congress knew that annexing Texas would mean instant war with Mexico, as indeed it did before the ink on the annexation treaty of 1845 was dry.

After Eli had fulfilled his obligation in the army, he and James Head started to Alabama to rejoin their families. While there, they again were drawn into a fight, this time with the Creek Indians who had joined forces with the

---

[130] McLean, *Papers*, Vol. 15, p. 152.

[131] McLean, *Papers*, Vol. 13, p. 50.

[132] McLean, *Papers*, Vol. 15, p. 157.

Seminoles in attacks on Alabama settlements. After the Creek were driven down into Florida, and after some coaxing of their kin, Eli and James convinced the families to return with them to the new nation of Texas.

This time, the Seales and the Heads both forsook northern Robertson County, where they had first settled, in favor of a lovely creekside prairie over which they had ridden several times on various journeys. They settled fifteen miles due east of Staggers Point on a strip of land in modern Brazos County that rose gently between two north-south creeks, Big Cedar Creek and Sand Creek. This area would become known as Seale's Neighborhood, and it is where Eli, Susannah, and several of their children would live out the rest of their days.

Some years later, Mary Lena Seale Stewart, a granddaughter of Eli's who lived on the property, wrote a short remembrance of life there that is poetically dense, evocative, and a rich glimpse of that life so different from ours and even then fading fast:

> I just feel like writing of the old days, about the old dug well in the hollow, with the old oaken bucket and the gourd we kept there to drink from, where we washed our clothes (Sister Rosie would hang all the little pieces on bushes and call them Christmas trees — the old gourd in hot water so much it was white and the water glistened in it); the old spring branch where the water ran glistening over limestone rocks where we kept our butter and buttermilk; the big peach orchards, and how we'd hitch old Pete to the slide and bring up a big box full at a time to dry, can and preserve; the big Hoss Apples — then was the time when Mother had no trouble getting John and me out of bed early, we each wanted to be first to the apple tree to pick up the apples that fell in the night before the

chickens got them — the big plum thickets, and the wild plums and grapes and persimmon thickets and the Muscadine Grapes and Muscadine preserves; the Black Haws and the Huckleberry pies...; the big Ribbon Cane patch; the syrup making and candy pullings; the deer hunting with the head light (Pap [Eli's son Joe] would go deer hunting in the day time, come home with a deer in front of him in the saddle; the lake muddyings and the fish fries that followed; turkey and duck hunting, and the little hickory nuts on Hickory Ridge; and all the carding, spinning and weaving; the quilting bees and log rollings with a big lunch and a party at night; the horse back riding (we rode side saddle then) and the rides in the old ox wagon with Old Ben and Lep, the wagon bed high at each end and sloped at center; the berry pickings and the bee robbing and the corn gathering in the Fall, and the big Rattlesnake Watermelons loaded on that grew in the corn field, (we had watermelon in the winter, had to heat them by the fire to warm them up to eat); and let's not forget the potato digging, the cotton chopping and picking that go with farming; and above all, the coon hunting with the dogs!

Once a year we'd pile the cornstalks in big piles and on a Saturday night our cousins ... would come over and we'd burn them.. Each would try to see who could set the most fires... We had the time of our lives playing hide and seek and other games.

We raised geese. I had to herd the goslings and keep them off ant beds. Mother made the best bread with a big goose egg. Sometimes we milked as many as thirty cows, fed the milk to our hogs, two or three dogs and eighteen cats! There was always a big dish of honey on the table, and, oh, the hog killings! with the spare ribs, long ropes of stuffed sausage, hog's head cheese, pigs feet fried in batter and cracklin' bread — nothing you get today tastes half so good — all cooked on a wood stove. We had lots of dried venison and methyglen [a kind of mead] to drink. Our ice came in burlap bags.[133]

If there was any one crop that laid the foundation of life in this part of the frontier — and all across most of the American frontier — it was corn. Every farmer grew it, and every family consumed it in a mind-boggling variety of ways. It was eaten fresh. It was made into cornbread that was eaten at virtually every meal with its own subtypes. As Victor Treat wrote:

You could cook it on, in, or under the fire, and it could be dry, moist, custard, sweet, hot, or greasy. It could be placed in a crock and soaked in lye water which would loosen the hull of the kernel, causing it to swell and thus become hominy. Hominy could be preserved and eaten as such, or it could be dried and ground into grits. An infinite number of techniques and recipes were utilized to prepare hominy and grits for the table.[134]

While wheat was used for biscuits, pie crusts, and pancakes, it was not a successful crop in Central Texas, and so wheat flour was imported and used sparingly. (Hence the settlers' diet was gluten-light if not gluten-free.) Biscuits

---

[133] Stribling, *Twixt the Brazos and the Navasot,* p. 40
[134] Treat, "Brazos County Agriculture," *Brazos County History*, p. 67.

were known as "Billy Seldom," while cornbread was known as "Johnny Constant."[135] Here, farms were built on three Cs: corn, cotton, and cattle.

One other detail of the above account that cries out for elaboration is the Southern practice of "lake muddyings" and subsequent fish fries. The fishermen would wade into lakes with cotton hoes, gigs, nets, and the greatest example of onomatopoeia in the English language: "splunges." Splunges were wooden planks about eight inches by six inches fitted onto hoe handles. Using the hoes and splunges, the fishermen would wade in kicking and stirring up the muddy bottom as they went. Soon the fish would begin jumping out of the water, at which point other non-splungers would use multi-pronged gigs attached to long a cane poles to stab the fish. As the water became muddier, the fish floated to the surface "gasping" for clean water to breathe. The perch appeared first, followed by bass, and finally bream. At this point, they were simply netted or grabbed by hand. The pioneers learned this method from Indians, who in turn, it is said, had learned it from watching bears. Thus was the saying "muddying the water" born.[136]

(Sportsmanship was no part of the hungry settlers' thinking; there were only means and ends, and if the end was food on the table, then the means was utterly irrelevant. This ethos extended into the modern era when fishermen in this region used electrical wires connected to a crank telephone to electrocute fish in rivers and streams. Catching these poachers was one of the tasks of Texas' earliest game wardens.)

Back at Staggers Point, for several years, Bettie and Robert lived a very prosperous life on the Little Brazos River. But to the southwest Santa Anna was reneging on the

---

[135] J. Frank Dobie, *Tales of Old-Time Texas*, (Austin: University of Texas Press, 1928) p. 8.

[136] Wayne Capooth —http://deltafarmpress.com/muddying-water-has-long-history-fishing-method

conditions of his surrender and still contesting the border and therefore, to all appearances, making a fool of Houston for having spared him. But Houston later defended his reasoning for letting the dictator live.

> It was on the night of the 21st and the early morn of the 22d when I was confined to my cot in camp, suffering from my wound. My mind was directed to the subject of how to secure the greatest good to Texas from the victory. Santa Anna and his command were overpowered and vanquished, it was true, but a large military force of the enemy, consisting of 5,000 troops, were advancing in battle array, within forty-eight hours march of my camp. Nor was Texas a free Republic....
>
> My motive in sparing the life of Santa Anna was to relieve the country of all hostile enemies without further bloodshed and secure his acknowledgment of our independence, which I considered of vastly more importance to the welfare of Texas than the mere gratification of revenge.[137]

History bore out that suing for peace instead of exacting revenge was the smarter path.

---

[137] *Writings of Sam Houston*, p. 10.

Last known photograph of Sam Houston, taken on or about March 18, 1863, four months before his death. Sixth plate daguerreotype possibly by J.H. Stephen Stanley of Houston. Houston's many detractors knew him simply as "Big Drunk." But his fans seemed to have gotten the last word. In Huntsville, where he last lived, there stands a 67-foot-tall statue of him. (The Egyptian Colossi of Memnon are but 60 feet.)

The uncertainty of the moment notwithstanding, there was now finally at least the hope of prosperity *and* peace. For Robert's service to the new republic, he had been granted nearly one thousand additional acres — six hundred acres in Hill County and three hundred acres in Brazos County.[138]

The revolution might have been over, but the less formal, larger, and more deadly war — the Indian war —

---

[138] Walker, *Brazos County History:* p. 23.

dragged on. According to one historian, the residents of Brazos County "set out to handle their own affairs to a great extent." It is not true that the settlers at Staggers Point and surrounding communities were merely rogue vigilantes. On April 23, 1838, Robert, William, and Hugh Henry, Eli Seale, James Head, James Dunn, the Fullertons, Millicans, and many other families of the area sent a signed petition to the Texas Congress asking for help:

> Your Memorialists residing high upon the Brassos and Navasotto Rivers, and from sad experience deeply feels the neglect of our government, in not providing some means to protect the exposed frontier — therefore your memorialists prays your honorable body to afford them some means of protection as speedily as the nature of the case will admit of, for your memorialists are daily and hourly exposed to the mercy of the merciless Savages. Our Surveyors have been murdered togather with their hands and within the last 2 days one of our Neighbors was inhumanly butchered and his scalp born off in triumph by the Indians, and they not meeting with opposition are dayly becomeing more insolent and bold and your memorialists being generally in Moderate circumstances are unprepared to follow the indians and retake the booty that they are carrying off together with the scalps of our Relatives and friends. [T]herefore your memorialists pray your honorable body to send some means to protect the frontier and drive back the Indians so as to enable your memorialists to complete their crops, and Your memorialists would respectfully suggist to your honorable body the vast importance of sending up a fiew pieces of Artillery, one at least to each dens[e] settlement togather with some of the

munitions of war, ... [W]ith great reluctance
your memorialists will be compelld to leave
their homes and crops without some speedy
and efficient means of protection is awarded to
them, by your honorable body, and if for want
of the necessary protection your memorialists
have to leave their homes ma[n]y of them no
doubt will continue on [to] the Land that gave
them birth and thereby Texas itself will
become weakened and the frontier become
entirely depopulated — whereas on the other
hand let the means of defe[n]se be afforded
and your memorialists will as in duty bound
ever pray &c.[139]

In other words: send us some cannon or we're leaving. No
cannon were sent.

Another historian added, "Whether they were compelled
to do so by their isolation or by their independent spirit, their
actions caused Sam Houston, while he was president of the
Republic of Texas, to tell representatives from the area that
he hoped the Indians would scalp them. Houston was
incensed at Texas' violation of Indian treaties and thought
some residents had been too zealous in efforts to protect
settlers."[140] One assumes the statesman was using hyperbole
to make a point. But either way, he got his wish.

It was now the fall of 1838.

Northeast of Staggers Point in modern Houston County,
darkness had just fallen on the Madden family's double-log
cabin, but the moon was full. The men were in one section of
the cabin, moulding bullets. The women and children were
on the other side, across the dog trot, making ready for bed.
In the gathering dark, Indians crept silently to the house and

[139] McLean, *Papers*, Vol. 16, p. 425.
[140] Walker, *Brazos County History*, p. 23.

listened, ascertaining who was in which room, and what they were doing.

Suddenly they let fly their blood-curdling scream and before the Maddens could reach for a weapon the Indians were in the dog trot, blocking both doors and so separating the men from their wives, mothers, and children. In the light of the fireplace on the women-and-children side, and with one Indian blocking the door by holding his arms up to the upper corners and his legs out to the bottom corners in a large X, the gruesome work of death methodically began. One mother was tomahawked in the body but fell in such a way that she rolled under a bed, and one of her little sons quickly followed her under. Another woman was tomahawked in the skull and fell head-first into the fireplace, bleeding so profusely that her final earthly act was to quench the fire. In the darkness now, the killing continued. Incredibly, the mother and son who had hidden beneath the bed crawled across the floor in the dark and escaped between the splayed legs of the brave at the door.

On the men's side of the cabin, trapped and possessing plenty of bullets but nothing with which to fire them, the men simply attempted to escape through the windows rather than go to the aid of their wives and children who were screaming only feet away. We are loathe to judge in such extreme situations, but by any measure it was an astonishing act of cowardice. Shouldn't one happily go to one's death making some kind of effort, even with bare fists, rather than live out his days in the guilt of such an abdication of basic duty?

One of the fleeing men met up with the mother and son who had escaped and made for the neighboring corn field, with an Indian in pursuit. When the settler plucked a corn stalk from the ground and held it to his shoulder like a long-gun, the Indian retreated, at which the settlers disappeared into a thick cane brake and watched as their cabin went up in flames. In what became known as the Eden-Madden Massacre, seven women and children had been slaught-ered.[141] [142]

106

Nationhood had brought no change in violence between settlers and natives, and it was getting closer and closer to home.

On New Year's Day, 1839, Stacy Ann Marlin Morgan sat with a few members of her extended family in fading light of dusk. They lived a few miles north of Staggers Point at the falls of the Brazos River, and Stacy Ann's husband had gone with some of the other men of the settlement down below the village of Bucksnort (Old Marlin) to buy corn. This left the older men of the families and the women and children at home. The women had finished their milking and the night's other chores, had eaten supper, and were sitting around the fire talking and carding wool. The oldest boy in the house, Jackson Jones, was reading to the family from a song book when he was interrupted by a blood-curdling war whoop. Through the door burst an Indian who shot Jackson through the head with an arrow. Fifteen Indians stormed the cabin. Adeline Marlin, sixteen, and Mrs. Jackson Morgan were immediately tomahawked.[143] Stacy Ann's parents and her son were tomahawked and scalped. Stacy Ann herself was partially scalped and left for dead outside of the house, but she rolled under the puncheon floor and kept quiet.[144]

Three children had been playing in the yard at dusk when they heard the whoop. They hid in the brush behind an old rail fence. Little Wesley Jones actually ran into the house, then fled unspotted by the Indians after seeing the carnage in progress. He was followed out by little Mary

[141] Wilbarger, *Depredations*, "The Maden Massacre," p. 211.
[142] Dana Goolsby "The Edens-Madden Massacre of Houston County" http://www.texasescapes.com/DanaGoolsby/Edens-Madden-Massacre-of-Houston-County.htm

[143] Moore, *Savage Frontier Vol. II*, p. 136.
[144] "Interview with Mr. Porter Mullins" Riesel, Texas U.S. Work Projects Administration, Federal Writers' Project (Folklore Project, Life Histories, 1936-39); Manuscript Division, Library of Congress.Copyright status not determined. Ada Davis, P.W., McLennan County, Texas, District No. 8, OCT 1 1937, WORKS PROGRESS ADMINISTRATION, SAN ANTONIO, TEXAS. Miss Effie Cowan, P.W.

Marlin. After the Indians had finished their work and left with a slave girl, who was never seen again, along with anything else of value they could find, Isaac, one of the boys outside, slipped into the house to see if anyone was still alive. He found, Adeline, her body in one place and her head in another, missing its "beautiful long golden hair."

Stacy Ann, hearing Isaac's footsteps on the floor above her, thought the band had returned and so kept silent. Isaac, thinking all were dead, ran seven miles through the night, to the settlement where his uncle John Marlin lived, arriving at daylight. The men hurried to the scene of the massacre to look for survivors and bury the dead.

When Stacy Ann was finally convinced the raiders were gone, she crawled out from under the floor and went into the black woods, without a portion of her scalp. The wolves howled around her as they could smell the blood of her wounds, and she expected to be ripped to pieces now even as she had survived the massacre. She passed out until the next afternoon, when she awoke thirsty and feverish. When some milk cows passed her on their way to a pool, she clung to the old bell cow's tail and held on until it dragged her to the spring, where she drank and where the men who had come to the scene of the massacre finally found her.[145] The following day the victims were buried "amid the wailings of their grief-stricken relatives and friends."[146]

---

[145] Moore, in *Savage Frontier,* says that Stacy Ann Marlin, "severely wounded, made her way to John Marlin's home around noon the following day." Vol. II, p. 137.

[146] Moore, *Savage Frontier, Vol. II*, p. 137.

Texas Tough: Stacy Ann Marlin Morgan, scalped but alive. In later years, she would sit in the corner of her cabin smoking a corncob pipe and retelling the story of her survival. For the rest of her life she wore a cloth around her head to hide the "bare white skin that finally grew over the top of her skull."[147]

When word of the Morgan massacre reached Staggers Point, the writing seemed to be on the blood-spattered wall. The men decided they must either defeat the Indians or retreat east and south to the greater safety of the Austin Colony. It was an understandable emotion but flawed logic, because there was always another Indian band moving in to take the place of the band that had just been killed or run off. The Staggers Point men, along with settlers in Wheelock and Old Franklin, chose to fight. On January 14, fifty-two men organized themselves and elected Benjamin Franklin

---

[147] Baker, History of Robertson County, p. 63.

Bryant as their leader. Bryant, over six feet tall with black sideburns, had come into Texas four years earlier from Alabama and had built a fort on the Little River named Bryant's Station. Among the minutemen were Robert's younger brothers William and Hugh, and possibly Eli's oldest son, Christopher Columbus "Clum" Seale.[148]

Four days later, on January 14,[149] some seventy Indians attacked Isaac's family, the Marlins, below the present town of Marlin. This time, however, several men were home, and they were prepared. They killed seven of the raiders and forced a retreat. A slave of Jarrett Menefee's by the name of Hinchey had been instructed what to do in case of such an emergency and ran "full speed and badly scared" more than twenty-five miles downriver to alert the next settlement.[150] It is said he covered the ground in about the same time a good horse might have.

Bryant's volunteers crossed the Brazos near Morgan's Point and traveled up the west side of the river. Soon they found a deserted camp with fresh signs. About a mile away, they picked up a fresh trail leading into Indian settlements. When the trail reached the river, they determined there were sixty-four fresh horse tracks and another trail of Indians on foot, all crossing the river.

The settlers followed the tracks until nightfall, when they spotted fire in the area of John Marlin's home. They left the trail and headed for the flames. They were relieved to find it was only a prairie fire.

The next day, January 16, the minutemen picked up the tracks of a large number of Indians and overtook them at Horn Hill, near modern Marlin in Falls County. They were the Anadarko, a subset of the Caddo people, seventy of them, led by Chief Jose Maria. Among them were also Ionies and Kichais.[151] Jose Maria, who possessed piercing eyes but was

---

[148] Smith, American Descendants. p. 272.

[149] Moore, *Savage Frontier, Vol. II,* p. 140.

[150] Baker, History of Robertson County, p. 63.

stocky and stood only five feet tall, took aim from his horse and calmly fired on the settlers, putting a bullet hole in the sleeve of one and thus opening the battle.[152]

Statue of Chief Jose Maria, Anadarko, Oklahoma

The minutemen charged them, but gunfire from the Indians drove them backward, and, in a bit of Napoleonic folly that would dominate warfare until the end of the Civil War, the men were ordered to form a line on the open prairie. The order was misunderstood as one of full retreat. As the settlers withdrew from the field, the Indians charged from the woods, firing their guns and screaming war cries. The disorganized settlers scattered, but still the Anadarko

---

[151] Moore, *Savage Frontier Vol. II*, p. 136.

[152] Smith, Rick L., Wild West, October 2002, Vol. 15 Issue 3, p20.

advanced. Bryant's men panicked and ran for their lives. Three settlers died in the first charge, and one was killed later. Jackson Powers was shot off his horse. When his brothers and fellow soldiers stopped and tried to put him back on the horse, the horse was so frightened that it plunged so they could not get him back on. He told them he knew he was killed and that they should leave him and save themselves. Jackson did die, and indeed his brothers lived.[153]

One Wilson Reed was knocked from his horse by a protruding branch. As he lifted his head from the ground and saw the Anadarko approaching with their tomahawks, he called out in a jocular bellow, "Oh Lord, boys, Mary Ann is a widow!" at which point he was scooped up and carried to safety by one of his fellow combatants.

Hugh Henry and Irish neighbor William Fullerton, William Henry's brother-in-law, stood back-to-back. They fought with guns. Then they fought with knives until they were both shot dead.[154]

When darkness fell, the remaining settlers escaped. It would be known to the settlers of Staggers Point as the Battle of Horn Hill but everywhere else as "Bryant's Defeat." Men from Old Franklin gathered the dead back to their town and buried them in the cold, hard January dirt.[155]

---

[153] Interview with Lizzie Wyche Powers, b. 1866.)
http://www.forttumbleweed.net/historymarlin.html

[154] On the website FindAGrave.com, Lindsay Hale Boyd writes that William Fullerton's wife might have been Margaret Henry, sister to the four Henry brother emigrants, in which case we have another case of double-in-laws: a Henry brother marrying a Fullerton and a Fullerton brother marrying a Henry. Lindsay Hale Boyd writes, "Margaret Henry was born in Ireland in 1810. She married William H. Wilson in Carolina in 1825 or 1826. She moved, a widow with three children, to Boligee, Alabama about 1829 or 1830. She married William Fullerton in Boligee on 2 August in a Presbyterian Church by Rev. Eleazor Harris. William Fullerton was killed in the same battle that took Hugh Henry's life. After Margaret's death in 1852 or 1853, Robert Henry was appointed guardian of her three remaining minor children, Margaret, Edward, and Robert. This record presents a strong probability that Margaret Henry was the sister of the Henry brothers, brought to America in 1822 by James Henry."

[155] Katherine Galloway, "Ghost Towns of Robertson County," 1975,

Did Bryant's minutemen even have the right Indians? It was a point of pride with Chief Jose Maria that he never killed a woman or child in a raid or battle and that he never sanctioned this. Such an ethic was not in evidence at the Morgan home, to put it mildly. For another thing, the January 9, 1838, issue of the *Telegraph and Texas Register* reported that the Morgan home had been attacked by about fifteen Indians, not seventy.[156] In light of these variances, it seems likely that Jose Maria's Anadarko were certainly guilty of the January 16 Marlin raid but probably not guilty of the New Year's Day Morgan massacre.[157]

The Anadarko had won the battle, but it was not a harbinger of things to come. Indeed, by the middle of the next decade, their numbers were tiny, and they were under such a constant threat of attack from the Waco and the Tawakoni that Jose Maria, in a foxhole conversion, suddenly became one of the biggest advocates for peace with the whites among all Texas Indians and turned to the new republic for protection. Years later, Jose Maria visited Benjamin Bryant at his station and offered him his pipe to smoke; Bryant insisted that Jose Maria should smoke first as he had won the battle, and the old chief proudly obliged.

In at least one case, the Staggers Point men — we don't know specifically who — did attack the wrong Indians, killing members of a group later deemed to have been peaceful.

This wild land had taken the baby of Robert's family, the

---

www.robertsoncounty.info

[156] Moore, *Savage Frontier Vol. II*, p. 137.

[157] Supporting but inconclusive evidence that these were indeed the culprits of the Morgan Massacre is found in the autobiography of George Washington Morgan: "Jose Maria an [deleted: Cado] Anadarco Chief commanded —the Indians Cados, Ionis, Anadarcos 64 in all, well armed the Kirkard & Gill Gun. They left one of these Guns at my father's house whom they killed 16 days before."(McLean, *Papers*, Vol. 8, p. 142.) It is also possible that the Morgan Massacre was carried out by Indians who fell in with Jose Maria's band within a few days afterward, a scenario that would explain both the gun left behind and Jose Maria's denial.

brother who had once marveled at that strangest of frogs, the "land terrapin." And while the Indian wars would drag on for more than three additional decades, there is no subsequent record of Robert leaving home again to fight in them.

The Henrys might have been done chasing Indians, but Indians were not done with the Henrys. Ten years after Bryant's Defeat at Horn Hill, Robert's brother William, next in age to him and on whose land the town of Staggers Point actually sat, was riding his horse home from a trip across the Little Brazos to the Dillard Community (now Mumford) to get groceries. He was hit by a poisoned arrow. He had to crawl for half a mile, but made it home with the food before he expired.[158] By 1849, of the three Henry brothers who quit Ireland for Texas,[159] two were dead at the hands of Indians. Land in Texas had not been free after all, but rather, for a random few, it had exacted the ultimate price.

---

[158] Galloway et al., "The Irish of Staggers Point," p. 12, p. 23. In other accounts, written by Sam Rice Jr., William dies of an infection from the arrow wound a few days after arriving home. In Baker's A History of Robertson County, it is written that William was "ambushed while leaving his boat on the Brazos carrying a load of groceries about at Fort Tenoxtitlan. He crawled home only to die a few days later from the deadly wounds made by the poison arrows." p. 320.

[159] Brother James Henry remained in Alabama until 1852, when he too moved to Staggers Point.

9.

Ascending the Arms of God,

or, Puss Webber's Wash Kettle

ALTHOUGH ELI SEALE WAS FAST APPROACHING fifty, his services as a soldier and ranger were still most welcome in the young republic. As the 1840s dawned, the push for settlement from the east was beginning to be echoed by another push from the north. Whites from the upper South braved the red hills and woods of Indian Territory to cross the Red River into north Texas. Now settlers along the Red River were under continual attack, and those farther down in the Three Forks area of the Trinity began to call on the republic to oust all Indians from the present-day Dallas-Fort Worth area.

In December 1840, the Texas Congress authorized a large force of volunteers to ascend the Brazos in pursuit of Indians, nearly all of whom were assumed to be hostile. General Edwin Morehouse, a New York native,[160] was to draw volunteer companies from Montgomery, Milam, Washington, and Robertson counties. He ordered his volunteers to rendezvous at Nashville-on-the-Brazos by January 25, 1841, for a campaign expected to last three weeks. The settlers were about to acquire some very unusual allies.

Chief Placido of the Tonkawa

Nothing in history would prove more disastrous for American Indians than the potent combination that blended Anglo organization and relentlessness with the enmity and tracking skill of rival Indian tribes and nations. About this time, Chief Placido of the Tonkawa tribe came into Houston and volunteered for this expedition. He told the military authorities that he had just come from a village on the upper Brazos where four hundred to six hundred Indians were congregated. Placido offered the services forty-seven

---

[160] Thomas W. Cutrer, "MOREHOUSE, EDWIN," *Handbook of TexasOnline* (http://www.tshaonline.org/handbook/online/articles/fmo42), accessed October 30, 2014. Uploaded on June 15, 2010. Published by the Texas State Historical Association.

warriors, who were then camped between Houston and Austin on a tributary of the Brazos. In return, Placido asked that his warriors be paid the same as the white soldiers, that they receive a share of the plunder, and that they have exclusive disposal of all Caddos and Kichais who might be taken in battle. The whites, he said, could have the Cherokees.

What the Tonkawas had planned for the Caddos and Kichais is not completely clear, but one fate of Tonkawa's enemies was well known. Cannibalism. The Tonkawas were one of two tribes in Texas known to eat their enemies. The Karankawas of the gulf coast were the other, and old Texans referred to these two groups as "Tonks" and "Cronks."

For the most evocative account of a Tonkawa cannibalism ceremony, during which a Comanche was eaten, once again we must turn to the incomparable memoir of Noah Smithwick:

> The only [ceremony] I ever witnessed was in Webber's prairie [east Travis County], the occasion being the killing of a Comanche, one of a party that had been on a horse stealing trip down to Bastrop. ... After killing and scalping him they refused to continue the chase, saying they must return home to celebrate the event, which they did by a feast and a scalp dance. Having fleeced off the flesh of the dead Comanche they borrowed a big wash kettle from Puss Webber, into which they put the Comanche meat, together with a lot of corn and potatoes, the most revolting mess my eyes ever rested on. When the stew was sufficiently cooked to allow its being ladled out with their hands the whole tribe gathered round, dipping it up with their hands and eating it as greedily as hogs. Having gorged themselves on the delectable

feast they lay down and slept till night, when the entertainment was concluded with the scalp dance.

Gotten up in all the hideousness of war paint and best breechclouts, the warriors gathered round in a ring, each one armed with some ear-torturing instrument, which they operated in unison with a drum made of dried deer skin stretched tightly over a hoop, at the same time keeping up a monotonous Ha, ah, ha, raising and lowering their bodies in time that would have pleased a French dancing master, every muscle seeming to twitch in harmony. Meanwhile some old hag of a squaw would present each in turn an arm or leg of the dead foe, which they would bite viciously, catching it their teeth and shaking it like savage dogs. And high over all waved from the point of a lance the scalp, dressed and painted, held aloft by a patriotic squaw. The orgies were kept up till the performers were forced to desist from sheer exhaustion.[161]

With Chief Placido's offer of help thought fair enough, he was sent to Nashville-on-the-Brazos to find Morehouse and offer his Tonkawas as scouts. The expedition organized at Nashville on January 25. Under Morehouse, Capt. George Erath, an Austrian immigrant, was authorized to take command of a spy company, and the Tonkawa were authorized to join this expedition. Erath became "Captain of Spies." There were about one hundred twenty-five whites in the party, a hundred "Tonks," and fifteen Lipans. He had charge of the Indians and about twenty white men for spies.

---

[161] Smithwick, *Evolution of a State*, pp. 179-181.

George Erath (1813-1891)

As of January 29, the boys were still at Nashville, where Col. Morehouse wrote an I.O.U. for pork and corn. A Robertson County spy company was placed under Sam Killough. Eli Seale was recruited into this company and rode as a "mounted gunman."[162] Eli might have been getting long in the tooth for living in the saddle and sleeping on the ground, but he wasn't the oldest in the company. Among Killough's other scouts was none other than Sterling Clack Robertson. At age fifty-six, the empresario of the Robertson Colony apparently felt like leaving command to a younger man and instead rode as a scout.

They ascended the Brazos, with oak forests and riparian jungles gradually giving way to the limestone outcroppings that heralded the northern boundary of the Central Texas Hill Country. Erath later wrote that the Morehouse

---

[162] Letter by Samuel B. Killough discharging Eli Seale, Seale Family Papers, 1841-1888, Daughters of the Republic of Texas Library at the Alamo.

expedition "went up the Brazos above Comanche Peak, [just south of modern Granbury] from there to the Trinity, and then back to the Brazos. As for the Morehouse Campaign's net result, ironically, the Indian scouts were the only ones who killed any Indians: two "all that were seen on the whole trip; no one on our side was hurt," reported Erath. He wrote candidly:

> The expedition was the mistake of military characters, newly arrived in Texas. They were of the opinion that Indians could be exterminated by carrying the war into their own country in the winter season, by finding their winter villages, destroying their provisions, and starving them out.
>
> Experience had already taught the Texas rangers that the Indians were quartered in their villages in the summer time only, eating what little agricultural produce they made, and that in cold weather they scattered to hunt and feast on bear and other wild animals.[163]

Although the rangers of this Morehouse campaign were basically "all dressed up with nowhere to go," the campaign did put on notice whichever Indian groups observed it at a safe distance.

On the way home, the expedition stopped on March 1, 1841, at Camp Stroud near the falls on the Brazos, where volunteers who lived in the upper settlements of Robertson and Milam counties were discharged. Captain Erath even excused himself. The remainder of the company disbanded on March 5 back at the original county seat of Robertson County and the northernmost town between the Brazos and Trinity, Franklin (now known as Old Franklin).

---

[163] Erath, *The Memoirs of Major George B. Erath*, p. 57-58.

On March 29, Eli Chandler organized the Robertson County Minute Men. This was a Texas Ranger's dream team; three of them — James Matthews, Eli Seale, and his best friend, James Head — each already had led their own ranger companies. Also in the unit were Daniel Boone Jr., son of America's most famous frontiersman, and Mordecai Boon Sr., Daniel Boone's nephew (despite the changing spelling of the surname).[164]

On the evening of April 1, Captain Chandler received intelligence that Indians had attacked and killed Stephen Rogers Jr. at his home on the east bank of the Navasota, then stolen eight of his horses.[165] Chandler immediately began recruiting for what would be known as the Lewis Expedition, which would run April 4-18. Once again the campaign would muster at Franklin. Chandler convened twenty-five men and struck out on a "forced march" to pursue the Indians. The Franklin-based rangers moved east of the Navasota. At about eleven o'clock on the morning of April 11, they spotted Indians, two miles ahead and driving the stolen horses. In his official report of April 16, Eli Chandler remembered:

> I immediately gave chase at full speed for the distance of seven miles, and was enabled to recover all of the horses back, and take one from the enemy.
>
> I am sorry to say that, from the jaded situation of our horses, and the start which they had, they [the Indians] were able to elude us. While we must regret their escape, it affords me pleasure, that from the perseverance manifested on the march, and in

---

[164] Christina L. Gray, "BOONVILLE, TX," *Handbook of Texas Online* (http://www.tshaonline.org/handbook/online/articles/hvb81), accessed October 06, 2014. Uploaded on June 12, 2010. Published by the Texas State Historical Association.

[165] Stephen L. Moore, *Savage Frontier, Vol. III: 1840-41*, University of North Texas Press: Denton). p. 220.

the chase, by every man under my command,
to believe that nothing is wanting, on the part
of this command, but a fair opportunity, to
sustain that character for chivalry, which is
always anticipated from Texan citizens.[166]

Chandler's minutemen were back in Franklin by April 16
with the recovered horses. Each man, regardless of rank,
collected seven dollars for each day of the campaign.[167]

Eighteen forty-one proved one busy year for Eli Seale. No
sooner than he had returned from his second ranging
campaign than the Texas Congress appointed him and four
others to form a committee to found a county seat for the
newly created Navasota County. The constitution stipulated
that the county seat must be within five miles of the county's
geographical center. There being no such town, the men set
out to find a suitable site. The committee, composed of Eli
Seale, J.H. Jones, William T. Millican, Joseph Ferguson, and
Mordecai Boon, Sr., found a one hundred fifty-acre tract that
was originally unbroken post oak forest, bought it from
Elizabeth and William Pierpont for $150, and deeded it to
the county on July 30. They named it Boonville after
Mordecai, nephew of Daniel Boone, and settlers began
building it around a public square, with space in the square
reserved for a county courthouse. The following year, the
name of Navasota County was changed to Brazos. Boonville
became a thriving community hub for the surrounding
settlements and a trade outpost to Houston. (The town was
located two miles northeast of the site of current Bryan, on
FM 158, known as Boonville Road.)

But 1841 was barely half over. Eli Seale and James Head
re-upped for yet another expedition under Chandler and

---

[166] Journals of the Sixth Congress, Republic of Texas, 3:412.
[167] Moore, *Savage Frontier Vol. III*, p. 221.

Erath. Erath wrote, "In July, Captain Chandler and myself made a corporation [and] proceeded with 102 men in to the Cross Timber." Adding a small group from Austin, the total unit numbered about one hundred twenty. Again the rangers moved slowly up the Brazos past Comanche Peak, but were plagued by illness.

What's more, and maddeningly, each Indian village they came to seemed to have been recently vacated. "We passed several evacuated towns of the enemy in the Cross Timbers," wrote Erath, "and our spies used every exertion to ferret out the grand village."

The Cross Timbers is a largely forgotten landmark of Texas but one that once was a major feature. Settlers described it as a strip of thick forest ranging from five to thirty-five miles wide that ran north and south through north Texas terminating at the top edge of what could be considered Central Texas. Its chief characteristic was the thickness of its undergrowth, which acted as a virtual wall between the more settled land to the east the Great Plains to the west. In fact, modern maps place the top of the Cross Timbers all the way in southeastern Kansas, then bring it down across Oklahoma and then into its main body, a varying but wide area of perhaps one hundred miles bordered on the east by Interstate Highway 35 and reaching down to about Waco.

By August 3, the expedition had made camp in what was then considered the upper edge of the Cross Timbers, some sixty miles above Comanche Peak. They sent out scouts and awaited word. If the spies failed to make any discoveries soon, the boys would have to return home from lack of food. Then a few Indians appeared near their camp. Erath was immediately dispatched to chase them with twenty men. Still searching for the trail, he divided his unit, taking some of the men with him and sending the rest with Lt. William Love of the Robertson County Minutemen. Being a former Robertson County resident and living just south of the county now, this was likely Eli's unit.

Erath found the trail and "pushed hard" down it as he pursued the Indians. And who was at the end of the trail but Chief Jose Maria, he of Bryant's Defeat just two years earlier. The chief was wounded and one of his warriors killed in the skirmish. Capt. Erath lost one man. Chandler believed some of these Indians were Cherokees because they spoke English well enough to taunt the Texans at a distance.

Perhaps Eli Seale was frustrated by the lack of "success," or perhaps he was receiving looks from Susannah, looks that said there was work to do at home — corn to plant or hogs to slaughter or young boys who needed a father. Whatever the case, Eli's riding and fighting days were over. From the British to the Comanche, from the Mexican to the Creek, to the Caddo, Eli had taken on all comers. Now it was time for him and his neighbors to get down to the business for which they had entered this wild territory — farming, ranching, and building a family's future.

10.

Sold South

IN 1840 A SLAVE TRADER CAME through the area. The Henrys bought three slaves, two adults and a child,[168] and they considered them "a godsend."[169]

It is, of course, impossible to reconcile the stain of so heinous an institution as slavery with an otherwise inspiring tale of courage and resourcefulness. It raises many troubling questions and bewildering contradictions in the modern soul: how could a family so fiercely attached to the ideal of freedom implicate itself in something that was its very antithesis? What possessed this immigrant family with no history with slavery, and with a fierce Calvinist work ethic, to say one day, "We sure would like to own some people so they could do our hardest work for us"? It taints every positive description of them with a darkening parenthetical: "She was an angel of mercy (and a slave owner)," "She was

---

[168] 1841 Navasota County Tax Rolls, Notes on Slavery in Brazos County, Bill Page, 1993.

[169] Murray, "Home Life on Early Ranches of Southwest Texas." One alternative source claims they bought their slaves in Alabama and brought them with them to Texas. While possible, this seems unlikely given the comparative quality of the sources.

known to the whole community as a courageous and generous soul (and a slave owner)," "He was a pillar of the community, a tireless volunteer (and a slave owner)."

Moreover, it would be one thing if, like many others, they did not consider their slaves fully human; however wrong the assumption, there would at least be a certain internal logic to it, as you could then lump slaves in with other creatures like draft animals that you also forced to work and didn't pay. But such was clearly not the Henrys' attitude. As noted, the Henrys were strict, "bluestocking" Presbyterians, who would allow no work on Sundays. This included their slaves. On Saturday morning, everyone doubled down on chopping wood, preparing feed for livestock, and cooking, because all work would cease from noon Saturday to Monday morning in observance of the Sabbath. What's more, they loaded their slaves up on Sunday and took them to church with them. You don't take horses and cows into church for the salvation of their souls; you only do that for full-fledged, soul-possessing humans.

Lastly, there was nothing intrinsic in the Irish mindset — or even in this family's — that destined them for slave ownership. In fact, there was a fifth brother, Alexander, who was the oldest of them all and who also left Ireland for America. But Alexander refused to move to Alabama or Texas because he would not live in a state that permitted slavery. The Fullerton, Wallace, and McMillan families all sent word to Texas that Alex had settled in Indiana. The brothers would never see each other again.[170]

Odious as the institution was, we're not well-served in our understanding of history by a simplistic conception of what this arrangement was like. Relationships were asymmetrical to be sure, but were also no doubt complicated and complex, even extending to a deep mutual affection between the white and black families as they watched each

---

[170] Smith, *American Descendants of James and Margot (O'Hara) Henry,* 1992, p. iv

other grow and suffer loss over the decades. On the Henry plantation, the white and black children played together. Some scholars believe that, perhaps ironically, racism was more acute among poorer, non-slave-owning whites than among slave owners. But perhaps this is not so ironic after all on the theory that prejudice is born of ignorance, and those who did not own slaves were the most ignorant of blacks. While the poor whites knew nothing of black people except that their wealthier neighbors owned them, the slave owners knew them intimately (indeed, often biblically), and so in a strange way were less likely to subscribe to the most virulent strains of racism, even as they participated whole-heartedly in the "peculiar institution," as Southerners called it.

It might be cold comfort to those who would rather take unqualified pride in the lives of their ancestors, but it is worth noting that when the Civil War ended and the Henrys' slaves were freed, not a single one, it is said, left the family.[171] We should be careful about making too much of this statement and hasten to add that even if true, the primary reason for this steady state surely was the utter dearth of opportunities for black people to advance socially anywhere within reachable distances. That said, in the narrative of Annie Day, we have the story of one Bryan slave who did leave after emancipation, and her list of grievances do reveal a life that contrasts with life on the Henry plantation:

> We first lived at Boonville. The woman that had me had a hotel, and a string of little houses 'bout a hunderd feet long, and the hotel and the houses was all burned down. We went over to Bryan and got a bigger hotel. When Bryan was started old Boonville went down fast. Just about all [the] folks moved to Bryan...
>
> ───── The woman what had me didn't treat me very

[171] Murray, "Home Life on Early Ranches of Southwest Texas."

well... She didn't hardly let me off the place. I never got to go to school or even to church. She never did give me no money, but she give me clothes and enough to eat. I never was on a farm.[172]

Day didn't know that slaves had been freed until a couple passing through Bryan in a stage coach stopped at the hotel. The couple informed her that she was free and didn't have to stay with the woman any longer. They offered to take her to Waco, and she quickly accepted. They told her to gather her belongings and "slip down the street and stand by the flagpole." Day did so, and the couple drove her to freedom.

But while freedom was an essential first step, it did not yield equality, or even justice, and overt racism not only persisted throughout the country for well more than a century but seemed even to deepen after emancipation. In 1896, Bryan was the scene of a triple lynching. Six months later, another black man was lynched on Main Street in front of First National Bank.[173] The last year there was not at least one lynching in Texas was 1925.

Slavery. Alas, it thrived on the deep moral confusion of that day — and all earlier days — around the issue of race, a confusion the Henrys and Seales, also slave owners, shared with many thousands of other "God-fearing," "freedom-loving" people who chose not to see the contradiction between their actions and their professed values. An 1829 edict granted Texas a one-year exemption from Mexico's ban on slavery, but President Anastasio Bustamante ordered that all slaves be freed in 1830. To circumvent the law, many Anglo colonists played semantic games, converting their

---

[172] *Brazos County History*

[173] Cynthia Skove Nevels, *Lynching to Belong*, (College Station: Texas A&M Press, 2007) p. 95.

slaves into "indentured servants for life."[174] By 1836 there were five thousand slaves in Texas among thirty thousand settlers.

Nothing illustrates this moral confusion better than a resolution from a mass meeting of the citizens of Robertson County during the confusing final days of the Civil War in May 1865. There the aggrieved attendees resolved that they would fight on to the last man because they were "determined to all die freemen rather than live all slaves."[175] To these citizens, then, slavery was not forcing someone to work in a field all day for no pay; the real slavery was when other people prohibited your doing that.

In all probability, the Henrys like many other families thought they were simply doing what had to be done to get by in the New World. What's more, such families probably thought that they were giving their slaves a fair deal: they were "paid" for their labor with food, clothing, shelter — and probably better than they'd get anywhere else, they rationalized.

It is an interesting thought experiment to envision yourself suddenly in a new land where all of your peers have people doing their hardest work for them, and where these workers can be had for the price of what we would pay for a car. Your life becomes exponentially easier — or exponentially more productive — with each one you acquire. Everyone else seems to have them, and your ultimate authority, the Bible, seems to permit it, or at least it is construed to by your pastors. As moderns judging our forebears in hindsight, we can hope or fantasize that we would have had a strong enough moral compass and be socially and morally progressive enough to stand aloof from the intense cultural and economic pressures of that time, and so to reject the practice. But this is a mental parlor game,

---

[174] Alwyn Barr, *Black Texans: A History of African Americans in Texas, 1528–1995* (2nd ed.), Norman: University of Oklahoma Press, 1996), p.15.

[175] *Tri-Weekly Telegraph*, Robertson County, May 5, 1865.

and the fact is that none of us can know what we would have done. Such a thought experiment humbles us, cautions us against excessive judgment of those hidden beneath the sod, and makes us wonder what current institution, questioned only by some, will be viewed by future generations as so heinous as to be the "slavery" of our own age. Many are the candidates.

Because international slave trading had been outlawed around the turn of the nineteenth century, all of slave traders' income would be made through domestic trading. From 1830 to 1840 nearly a quarter of a million slaves were transplanted across state lines.[176] The period of the Henrys' purchase — in which vast numbers of slaves were moved from the Upper South to the Deep South and west eventually to Texas following an agricultural boom — would have fallen into what historian Ira Berlin coined "the Second Middle Passage."[177] He named it this because it reproduced many of the same horrors as the original Middle Passage, the transportation of slaves from Africa to North America. This large migration of slaves caused indescribable hardship. In 1820 a slave's child in the Upper South had a thirty percent chance of being "sold south" by 1860.[178] No doubt chief among those horrors was the breaking up of families. Slave traders had no economic incentive to buy or transport intact families, because in the early years, only young male slaves were in demand by planters for heavy labor.

The trader that came through Robertson or Brazos counties might have come up from Galveston but probably had ridden overland from New Orleans, which was then the largest slave market in America. Traders migrated over established routes using a network of slave pens, yards, and warehouses to house the slaves. As the journey advanced,

---

[176] Marcyliena H. Morgan *Language, Discourse and Power in African American Culture*, (Cambridge: Cambridge University Press, 2002), p. 20.

[177] Berlin, Ira. *Generations of Captivity: A History of African American Slaves.* (2003)

[178] Berlin, *Generations of Captivity*, pp. 168–69.

some slaves were sold and new ones bought. The slave trading firm League and Andrews Company of Houston was the source of early supply for farmers in Robertson County, according to one local history.[179]

Once the trip ended, slaves would face a life on the frontier as different as the pioneers had, a life of backbreaking work they might not have been accustomed to like clearing trees or plowing virgin fields. As in both Staggers Point and Seale's Neighborhood, new plantations were located in or near river bottoms for timber and river travel, which meant mosquitoes and other diseases would take large numbers of transplanted slaves whose immunities had developed elsewhere.

While there were a few families in the area with slaves in the dozens, the poor, clay-bound soil prevented the kind of large-scale, slave-intensive farming one found in the Mississippi delta. This meant that most of the families who did own slaves were like the Henrys and Seales, who owned them in two's and three's. County tax records show Eli's daughter Mary Ann Seale, bought a single twelve-year-old named Leroy.

<hr>

[179] J.W. Baker, *History of Robertson County*, p.128.

Mary Ann Seale Butrill, Eli and Susannah's daughter

For the Henrys, the slaves were a force multiplier for the family's own prodigious labor and probably did not shorten their own long workdays much. The slaves enabled Robert to expand his cotton crop and more easily care for the livestock. Slaves dug the well that remained in service for more than 140 years.[180] Bettie now had help in the house. Lint cotton was carded, spun, and woven into cloth. Along with wool, this supplied nearly all the clothing for the family and its slaves. While spinning and weaving was time consuming, the hardest job after the picking itself was separating the lint from the seed, but this was something the children could do, and every child — black and white — each night had to pull out enough seeds from the lint to fill his or her shoes before they could go to bed.

Robert, or "Squire Henry," as he was often called now due to his leadership within the community, built the first horse-powered cotton gin, or "horse gin," in that part of the country in 1850[181] on the edge of Red Top Prairie. There was no end to the children's rejoicing when they learned their seed-pulling days were over. The horse gin — an interesting

---

[180] Jimmie Henry Rice, *The Hearne Democrat*, June 6, 1968, p. 6.

[181] "Benchley," *Handbook of Texas*

contraption in the mold of numerous horse-powered machines of the age, including grain separators and saw mills — consisted of a portable treadmill. It resembled a small wagon that was slightly inclined at the front with a wood-planked treadmill making the floor and railings all around. The horse would be led up the ramp, closed in from behind, and the treadmill then unlocked, thus forcing the horse to walk to keep its balance. The treadmill turned a large flywheel resembling an oversized wagon wheel attached to the side of the machine, which by way of a long leather belt would turn down to a small axle on a separate machine sitting on the ground behind or in front of the treadmill. This created a high rate of revolutions per minute that could drive all sorts of ingenious machines. Some treadmills were large enough to fit two horses abreast, thus creating a two-horsepower motor (though probably a little more due to the incline). As they had from classical antiquity, horses and mules also were used to turn capstans and to do any number of chores on a circular lead. In this part of the country, mules and horses were led in circles to crush sugar cane for syrup.[182]

The Henrys and their slaves and tenants left a lot of blood, sweat, and tears on their plows in an effort to farm the land. But as years go by, one reads less and less about their "farm" and more and more about their "ranch." The inescapable fate of the land was cast by its geology. And the promise of the prairies near the Brazos, in what would later be called "The Claypan" would never pan out for farming, as the soil would not drain properly. Throughout the 20th century and until this writing, the land was leased to oil and gas companies. As early as 1937, Ola Maye Henry wrote that "one sharp descendant has exclaimed, 'The Lord must have put something under it, for He knows nothing will ever grow on it.'"[183] The fact that the state of Texas located its premier

---

[182] Smith, *American Ancestors of James and Margot (O'Hara) Henry*, p. 24.

[183] Ola Maye Henry, *The Hearne Democrat*, July 2, 1937.

agricultural university, Texas A&M, on this spot (by the heroic efforts of the Father of Brazos County, Harvey Mitchell) is perhaps the first and ultimate "Aggie joke."

Land was no longer free, but it was cheap, and Squire Henry secured more over time. Aside from the split-rail corrals and pens common on the frontier, it is said there was not a fence during his lifetime. His rapidly increasing cattle were branded *RH*, but they were not worth much. He tried to sell them, but they always seemed to die. Little did he know they were infested with cattle ticks. (It was his grandson, Robert Henry Seale, who, decades later, finally eradicated the ticks.)[184]

Robert decided to try sheep and bought some in Washington County to the south. During 1839 and 1840 this went well. He used slaves as shepherds. He sheared once or twice a year and sold the wool in Houston, saving back enough to supply the family in clothing.[185]

Horse sales were the next best to sheep. Their horses always went to the Brazos River bottom to spend the winter but returned in the spring. It was warmer down there out of the prairie wind, and they kept fat on mesquite grass and wild rye. He always supplied the preacher with a horse, and when once one was killed, Robert said, "Don't worry, I'll give you another one." [186]

Most of the settlers in the area also raised and relied on fowl — chickens, of course, but also guinea fowl and geese.

But it was hogs that yielded the greatest profit of all. They ran wild and fattened on post oak mast (acorns), so the only cost of production was the time spent in marking them by a crop under each ear and taking them to market. He got three cents a pound for them at Calvert, a seven-day round

---

[184] Murray, "Home Life on Early Ranches of Southwest Texas."
[185] Murray, "Home Life"
[186] Murray, "Home Life"

trip. Because they were so wild, driving them to market was considered the hardest job in the Henry portfolio. The management of such an undertaking required the utmost skill, and Robert always tried to secure the services of one Wesley Jones, whom he considered the best, to manage his drove, which usually numbered about three hundred five- and six-year-olds. He also sold pork to the Germans at New Braunfels.[187]

But they held back some hogs for consumption at the farm itself. The ones they picked for their own table they culled from the herd, penned, and fattened on "clabber," the frontier version of cottage cheese. [188] The Scots-Irish called it "bonnie clabber."

When the weather turned cool, it was time for hog-killing day. The men and women of Staggers Point and Seale's Neighborhood would rise early and light fires under huge iron cauldrons of water. When everyone was in place, they would stun the hogs, probably with clubs, then string them up by the hind legs to a rafter or a low branch, slit their throats, and drain their blood into buckets to be used for other purposes, probably including fertilizer. The hogs were then dropped in the boiling water to loosen their bristles, which were then scraped off. Once the carcasses were scraped clean, the hogs were gutted, and their entrails were laid out on tables for the women and children to separate and clean, squeezing out the intestines to prep them for their next life as sausage casings.

Meanwhile the men were carving up the meat, trimming the fat, rubbing it with salt and spices, and carrying it to the smokehouse. As the saying went, "nothing was wasted but the squeal." And so the trimmed fat was melted down in another pot and used to deep-fry bits of meat and skin known as "cracklings." The feet were pickled. And all manner of

---

[187] Murray, "Home Life"

[188] Victor H. Treat, "Brazos County Agriculture," *Brazos County History*, p. 66.

other culinary atrocities such as gelatinous headcheese and bloodcheese were prepared. Aside from setting the families up with protein and fat for months to come, the hog killings were social events that offered welcome relief from lonely field work, and they sometimes lasted a month until all the meat for the winter had been "laid by."[189] (Speaking pioneer is impossible with mastering the prepositions: While meat was "laid by" for the winter, supplies were "laid in" for a journey, and vegetables were "put up" for canning, while potatoes were stored "down-cellar.")

As the eventful decade of the 1830s drew to a close, the two youngest Henry children, Ann and Alexander, died, one after the other. This time the cause was malaria. Few if any realized at the time that the mosquito was to blame, but they knew it had something to do with the river. "The small farmers preferred the uplands where they could find cheap land, wood, and water," wrote one area historian. "They feared the river lands that they thought emanated miasmic mists and odors detrimental to health. The mosquito was not then recognized as the carrier of malaria and yellow fever." The rich soil along the river and the everlasting supply of water had come at too high a price.

In a slight retreat from their westward advance of thousands of miles, Robert and Bettie decided to move three miles back to the east from the river up onto a prairie they would name "Red Top" for the rusty color the grass took on in autumn. They built on a site where they would live the rest of their lives and that would stay in the family for more than a century and a half to come. The home would be modest to us, but to them it was a proud step up: a double-log house, likely with square-hewn instead of round logs. There were two big rooms with a dog trot between them, a small room in back of each of the large rooms, and deep porch stretching

---

[189] Victor H. Treat, "Brazos County Agriculture," *Brazos County History*, p. 66.

across the entire front. The house was heated by huge fireplaces in the ends of each of the big rooms. As was the common practice on the frontier, the kitchen was built in the back yard, keeping the house cooler in summer and mitigating the risk of burning the house down. Robert dug a well near the house that was used for more than a century.

Solid walnut furniture made in Huntsville was brought over by wagon. But for the most part, the lifeline to civilization for the whole area was a soggy wagon trail that ran southeast for one hundred miles to Houston. Almost everything that was not made on site came from there. As Jim Boyd writes, "Men in [Seale's N]eighborhood would take turns driving big freight wagons with six yoke oxen... They would leave for Houston loaded with cured meat, hides, molasses, cotton and other farm products. They would return loaded with flour, sugar, coffee, salt and other goods. Flour and sugar came in large barrels. Salt came in large sacks as did coffee, which was still green and had to be parched and ground. When Eli and James Head took the wagons to Houston, they would bring back shoes, pants, shirts, dresses, and everything else that the families needed."[190] (These freight wagons were in contrast to the other popular vehicle of the time, the "carryall," which despite its name carried much less than a wagon; carryalls were light-weight four-wheeled carriages usually seating four people and pullable by a single horse. The name was a corruption of the French *cariole*.)

Here in the Claypan, their dreams were coming together. They were farmers and ranchers in a new world. But through need or through compulsion, they would become much more.

---

[190] Boyd, *Grandfather's Journal,* p. 49.

STAGGERING

11.

Other Duties As Assigned

IF YOU ASKED A SETTLER in 1830s or 1840s Texas what they did for a living you probably would be greeted with a blank stare. It would have gone without saying that everyone was a farmer.

But while it would be accurate to call Robert, Eli, Bettie, Susannah, or any of their neighbors "farmers," it would also be a grossly insufficient description of their careers. No one, it seemed, did only one thing, even something as diverse and demanding as running a frontier farm and ranch. Oh, here and there existed a rare specialist — maybe a blacksmith or a gunsmith or a mason who specialized in fireplaces and chimneys.

For his part, Robert was also a surveyor, that being a growth industry on the frontier. While "surveying" to us conjures up a comfortable civil engineering career, in frontier Texas, surveying was among the most dangerous professions anyone could choose. Indians quite correctly saw survey parties as emblematic of all that threatened their way of life and their free range over the prairies and forests. And because surveyors by their nature worked along the outermost fringes of settlement, Indians attacked them frequently.

To our eyes the instruments, language, and even measures of frontier surveying seem alien and primitive. The tools of the trade were chains, stakes, and shovels with which to build mounds if there were no notable trees with which to mark a boundary. Boundary lines were articulated in deeds like this one, relating to Eli's land. First was the ceremonial the wind-up:

> In the Name of the Republic of Texas, to all whoom these presents shall come Know ye, I Sam Houston, President of the Republic aforesaid by virtue of the power vested in me by Law and in accordance with the Statutes of Said Republic in Such case made and provided do by these presents grant to H. G. Cattlet assignee of Young P. Alsbury, his heirs or assigns forever three hundred and twenty acres of Land Situated and described as follows in Brazos County Known as Survey No 25 on Sandy Creek waters of the Navisoto [sic].

Then, the perimeter was described:

> Begining at the South corner of No 14 on the North West Line of Survey No 16 for the East corner of this Survey, a Stake from which a post oak 15 in dia bars North 24 degrees West 8 varras and another Post Oak 12 in in dia bars South 84 degrees East 14 varras Thence South 45 degrees West at three hundred and fifty varres to the west corner of Survey North at twelve hundred a Stake from which a Post

oak 14 in dia bars South 13 degrees West 11 varres and another Post Oak 16 in dia bars North 11 degrees East 3 varres Thence North 45 degrees East... and three varres to the place of the beginning."[191]

With precision like that, it's no wonder disputes were common, but it did the job in most cases. The *vara* (along with the "cordel," the "league," and the "labor") was a holdover from Spanish colonial days and was just longer than a yard.

On top of farming, ranching, and surveying, it seems Robert was a habitual civic volunteer. In 1837, Robert was called to Wheelock, by Mr. Eleazar Louis Ripley Wheelock himself, to consider helping found the state's first university. His neighbors to the immediate north were contemplating "an ambitious educational institution to be known as Texas University." The fifteen men who met on May 10 drew up the institution's constitution and jointly conveyed a labor of land including the city of Lamar "for the purpose of promoting education and disiminating [sic] Knowledge upon correct and liberal principals [sic], entirely Republican." (They could have used a good university, or even a public grade school.) Those who gave one hundred dollars or a labor of land became stockholders. Shedding light on the general moral climate of the area, the constitution forbade "tippling and dram shops (bars), gambling houses, billiard tables, and disorderly establishments" in Lamar, although the hotel keeper might "furnish liquors to travelers." Texas' nascent Congress never granted them a charter, and the project quietly disappeared.[192] The University of Texas would not open for another forty-six years.

---

[191] Seale Family Papers, 1841-1888, Daughters of the Republic of Texas Library at the Alamo.

[192] Lelia M. Batte, *History of Milam County*, Texas, (The Naylor Co., 1956), p. 179.

In 1836, Robert was elected justice of the peace for the Second Precinct of then-enormous Milam County[193] and held court under shade trees. Justices of the peace were the lowest level in the new republic's Department of Justice, and so were used, as they are today, for duties like issuing marriage licenses and resolving lower-level civil disputes. But the following year, his duties would extend into a bigger controversy.

On June 12, 1837, the Texas Congress passed an act making it the duty of all "empresarios, commissioners, political chiefs, alcaldes, and other persons, to deliver over to the commissioner of the general land office, all titles, surveys, books, papers, documents or other things in their possession or charge belonging to this republic..." Texas' new land commissioner was John Petit Borden, but Texas was a big state, and he couldn't gather all the requisite documents himself in a lifetime of trying. Land documents in Robertson's Colony had naturally been the possession of Mr. Robertson. And since Sterling Robertson was then serving in the Senate, it might have seemed an easy enough task for Borden to pop over and ask Robertson for the land records of his erstwhile colony. But both men were flinty, and Borden didn't trust the combative one-time empresario. Moreover, Borden must have known that at least some of the documents he needed from Robertson had left behind in the care of one Ann Cavitt, who was an innkeeper on the San Antonio Road at Wheelock. On October 24, Commissioner Borden wrote Robert, instructing him to go to Mrs. Cavitt's inn in Wheelock to collect the documents, and also to the home of Thomas Hudson Barron, and to the home of John Goodloe Warren Pierson, then living in Washington County, to get all land documents they had. He also authorized Robert to pick up any documents he found along the way that might pertain to land ownership. When he had them in hand,

---

[193] Parker, *Recollections of Robertson County*, p. 165.

he was to have them delivered to the capital, Houston.

Borden wrote Cavitt and E.L.R. Wheelock asking them to convey all "important letters" to Robert. Ann Cavitt handed over all she had to Robert. In duplicate, Robert wrote her a receipt for all she had given him:

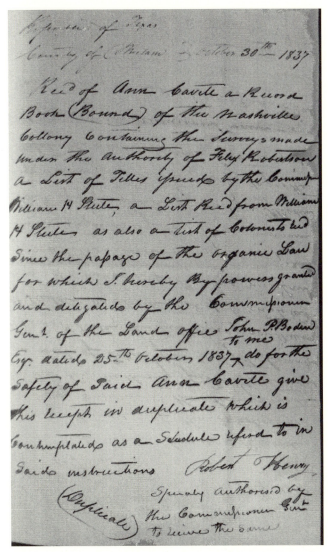

Receipt from Robert Henry to Ann Cavitt, October 30, 1837

Republic of Texas,

County of Milam,

October 30th, 1837

Rec'd of Ann Cavit, a Record Book (Bound) of the Nashville Collony containing the Surveys made under the Authority of Felix Robertson a list of titles issued by the Commissioner William H. Steele, a list rec'd from William H. Steele has also a list of colonists rec'd since the passage of the organic law for which I hereby by powers granted and delegated by the Commissioner Genl of the Land Office John P. Borden Esq. dated 25th October 1837 to me do for the safety of said Ann Cavitt give this receipt in duplicate which is Contemplated as a schedule referd to in said instructions

Robert Henry

Specaly Authorised by The Commission Genl to receive the same

(Duplicate)

Following this page there are two blank pages, and then a fourth page with the following mysterious sentence: "Mrs. I wish, you, to build a house near the Spring."[194]

But collecting from the others wasn't as easy as it might have seemed. On November 7, Robert wrote Borden from Milam, the former seat of Robertston's Colony, saying:

proceeded to the House of Capt Thomas H

---

[194] McLean, *Papers*, Vol. 16, p. 215.

> Barron and Demanded the Books & papers
> which he had in his posesion and he Refused
> to give them and stated to me that the[y] were
> of no youse to any Person so I could not get
> them. I have had no opportunity of seeing
> Majr Pierson yet But as soon as I can see him
> I will get what papers He Had and either take
> them down my self or send them down as soon
> as possible.
>
> Yours Respectfully
>
> Robert Henry[195]

Robert never got the Pierson papers either, but by November 20, he had personally ridden the one hundred miles to Houston to deliver the papers to Borden. Borden's letter of that date states that Robert had collected thirty-five surveys made in 1826 mostly of land lying within Leftwich's Grant, as well as the names of one hundred twenty-eight applicants for land in that grant. He was compensated for his "time and trouble in bringing the said register to this place."[196] [197]

In 1838 Robert was re-elected "Associate Justice" [of the Peace] "for the First Company of Militia."[198] In the same election, held in William Henry's home at Staggers Point, the community voted to establish the county seat of newly formed Robertson County at Franklin, known today as Old Franklin.[199]

That same year Robert helped to build a Grange hall at

---

[195] McLean, *Papers*, Vol. 16, p. 225.

[196] McLean, *Papers*, Vol. 16, p. 235.

[197] From this same collection of papers, on December 2, 1837 the Texas Senate records that "... Mr. Horton, from the Committee on claims and accounts, reported their rejection of the claims of Robert Henry." We do not know what claim he had made. (McLean, *Papers*, Vol. 16, p. 256.)

[198] McLean, *Papers*, Vol. 16, p. 69.

[199] McLean, *Papers*, Vol. 16, p. 71.

Staggers Point. The Grange was something like a cross between a Masonic lodge for farmers, a labor union that lobbied for favorable regulations, and a social club. The year 1838 predates the founding of the national Grange by more than thirty years, so likely it was a lowercase prototype of what would become the national organization. Robert was the keeper of the records, a post his son Hugh eventually inherited. By the time the statewide Grange got organized in the 1870s, it had a long list of initiatives and issue stances. These were in the future, but they reveal something of the mindset of the frontier planter and the trajectory of his politics. And to us they appear as an odd comingling of the progressive and the conservative:

In an indignant report they complained that at the Agricultural and Mechanical College "eighty-three boys are studying Latin and Greek, only three are studying agriculture"; they recommended a special school for training young women in the domestic arts (This eventually became Texas Woman's University.); they resolved that agriculture would be taught in the rural schools; the uniformed text book law was their brainchild.

Their resolutions at state meetings range from the common sense and progressive to the head-shakingly reactionary and meddling: to sell cotton only direct to the manufacture; to send only farmers to the legislature; to quit purchasing for the public schools any books published by Harper & Co. and to substitute in their stead the books of D. Appleton & Co.; to establish a cooperative bank; to manufacture all implements used on the farm; to establish a state fair; to endow a newspaper; to plant only one-third of one's crop in cotton; to forward farm products by the shipload direct to England and to purchase manufactured products in England by shipload in return; to establish a life insurance company; to establish a fire insurance company; to erect cotton compresses on the lines of all the railroads; to limit the amount of cotton to be planted by tenants, vagrants, and convicts; to establish a model experimental farm near

Austin; to buy only Texas-made wagons; to pass a Sunday law; to oppose a division of Texas; to reduce the consumption of intoxicating liquors; to adopt compulsory education; to adopt women's suffrage; to fortify Galveston and deepen its ports; to levy a heavy tax on luxuries and remove them from necessities.

As for the social aspect, which would have been very evident in the Henrys' day, historians Benedict and Lomax wrote:

> Probably the greatest advantage the Grange possessed for its members was the opportunity its weekly meetings gave for social intercourse. The local lodge meeting, held perhaps at some lonely schoolhouse, was often made the occasion for an all-day picnic. People came for miles, bringing their entire families. During the secret exercises curtains were spread over the windows and the children and non-members were excluded. The discussions and literary exercises were, however, open to all, and at noon the contents of large lunch baskets were spread on the grass under the trees outside of the building. To many people the Grange served as the principal means of social intercourse with their neighbors.[200]

Not having enough to do, Robert and son Hugh Reed Henry were also active Freemasons of Robertson County.[201]

Likewise, Robert's fellow patriarch Eli was routinely called on and elected to carry out myriad duties. In addition to having founded the Brazos County seat, Boonville, Eli served as the foreman of the first grand jury in the county,

---

[200] H.Y. Benedict, John A. Lomax, *The Book of Texas*, Garden City, N.Y.: Doubleday, Page, and Co., 1916) p. 306.
[201] Parker, *Recollections of Robertson County*, p. 220.

but the jury heard no cases in the first full year of service, as there were no crimes committed, or at least none reported.

But no one embodied the frontier jack-of-all-trades like the man who would become Boonville's most famous resident and eventually known as "the father of Brazos County," Harvey Mitchell. Mitchell came to the area from Tennessee as a young man and in 1841 was hired by Eli as a tutor for his children. The following year he moved to Boonville and, as one historian puts it, "apparently he had such a great sense of civic responsibility and such vitality that his undertakings became multidimensional." At twenty, he was chosen as the first deputy for the County Clerk's office, and he also served as deputy to the county judge, treasurer, and tax collector. He was superintendent of public instruction and supervised the building of the first hewed-log school. He ran all of these offices virtually single-handedly for almost a decade, during which time he also acted as justice of the peace. He even issued his own marriage license so that he could wed Jane Foley, the sister of Hugh's wife, and so became Hugh's brother-in-law, tying the Henry and Seale families together in yet another way. He was postmaster, blacksmith, and, oh yes, hotel proprietor. One wonders if anyone else actually lived in Boonville, or if it was all the creation of his own eccentric mind. He helped build local churches and became a trustee. He was a Mason and organized a lodge in Boonville of which he was installed as the first "Worshipful Master." At thirty-four, he moved his family to Red Top near the Henrys. Harvey later returned to Boonville. A major parkway through Bryan and College Station now bears his name. (In 1858, the first state money was received in Robertson County when $2,181.60 was deposited with the county treasurer. The county's minutes listed the teachers who were employed, their location and the number of children assigned to each. The teacher for Staggers Point was Mames Wilson. Students: 10. Between 1850 and 1860, the population in Robertson County had quintupled from 1,000 to more than 5,000.)[202]

Harvey Mitchell, 1821-1901

Of course, Bettie too would have had a long resume if the concept of "career" were any part of their conception of life. Fehrenbach summed it up this way: "Men were farmers, fathers, hunters, and soldiers. Women inherited all the incredible backbreaking labor of the primitive frontier."[203]

Perhaps one reason for Bettie's popularity was that among her many other jobs was that of folk doctor and midwife. The nearest trained doctor was in Houston, about one hundred miles away. "Aunt Bettie," as she became affectionately known, became the de facto doctor for the settlement. For bruises, she used a medicine she called "pidlock," brought from Ireland[204] along with other seeds,

---

[202] Baker, *A History of Robertson County, Texas*, p. 230.

[203] Fehrenbach, *Lone Star*, p. 89.

[204] "Pidlock" does not appear in reference sources. This may be a corruption of "burdock," a plant that was a common remedy in Irish herbal medicine. Burdock root can be a diuretic or soothe aching joints. Traditional Chinese

roots, herbs, and formulas.[205] She was known as a proverbial "angel of mercy" to the surrounding community, and, judging from the gifting of the Indian women on the occasion of her Elizabeth's birth, perhaps some Indians as well. If the sick were not able to come to her, she would travel to them regardless of the conditions, weather or otherwise.

On one such occasion, after the rest of the family had gone to bed, word reached her of a sick neighbor on Thompson Creek seven miles away. She would not wait for morning but, gathering her medicines and salves, mounted her horse and set out in the dark. She was riding bareback, and sidesaddle while holding her own small baby. (She *always* had a small baby.) The black mare she was riding was also a mother, and her colt was dutifully following. As they passed through a wooded stretch, a panther leaped from a tree branch to attack the colt. The mare responded in kind, pawing, biting, and kicking the big cat. The panther attacked time and again as they hurried ahead through the woods. Shooing the cat with her wide skirts and hissing at it, Bettie held the panther at bay until they drew close to the neighbors' house just before dawn. Soon the neighbors' dogs came out to meet Bettie. The dogs chased down the panther and killed it. Bettie, having done a piece of riding worthy of any rodeo champion, continued on her way, took care of the patient, and returned home safely. The family of the afflicted skinned the cat and preserved its hide.

The Henrys were renowned for their generosity and

---

healers used burdock root in combination with other plants to make cures for colds, measles, throat pain, and tonsillitis. The seeds of the plant contain beneficial fatty acids. The oil from the seeds can be used as a diaphoretic, which leads to increased perspiration, claimed to cleanse the body of toxins. According to traditional healers, diaphoretics are integral to treating influenza, gallbladder or liver disorders, and to aid the kidneys which purify the blood. http://www.naturalherbsguide.com/burdock.html

[205] Betty Westbrook Trant Family Papers, p. 2.

hospitality. It was easier to entertain now with the household help, and "Aunt Bettie" was an excellent manager. She trained some of the slaves to card, spin, weave, and sew, while others cooked, washed, and ironed. One slave named Mary Jane Taylor lived in Bryan into her nineties, and a family account says her voice was smooth and clear ... "as she spoke the old time true English which she learned from her mistress, and it is a very striking and interesting mark of distinction." According to the account, Taylor remembered Bettie as "a general, always in command using kindness, but requiring exactness of speech and work."[206]

They had moved away from civilization, but civilization was catching up to them. By the 1840s Staggers Point had three stores, a racetrack, and a gun club.[207] [208]

So why was the point named "Staggers"? The historical marker on Old San Antonio Road reads: "Community name, meaning 'Strivers Point' in dialect, was probably given for rugged zeal of settlers in face of hardships." Others have made a joke out of the English meaning of "staggers" and wondered aloud if it might refer to the Irish reputed penchant for alcohol. (Ask Whiskey Jim.) And still others called it "Staggers Pint."[209]

The dialect referred to would have been Ulster Scots. By the time the Irish reached Texas, their accents and dialect might already have been tempered by a decade of contact with American Southerners, but they would still have had a distinctive brogue. A good sample of the Ulster Scots dialect, which would have dominated in the Londonderry area in 1800, is found in this poem:

---

[206] Betty Westbrook Trant Family Papers, p. 3.

[207] "Benchley, Texas" *Handbook of Texas.*

[208] The race track and the gun club were said to have been located on George Dixon's land. *Bryan Daily Eagle,* November 30, 1967.

[209] Jimmie Henry Rice, *The Hearne Democrat,* September 22, 1961, p. 8.

"The Muse Dismissed"

by Hugh Porter (1780-1839)

Be hush'd my Muse, ye ken the morn
Begins the shearing o' the corn,
Whar knuckles monie a risk maun run,
An' monie a trophy's lost an' won,
Whar sturdy boys wi' might and main
Shall camp, till wrists an' thumbs they strain,
While pithless, pantin' wi' the heat,
They bathe their weazen'd pelts in sweat
To gain a sprig o' fading fame,
Before they taste the dear-bought cream—
But bide ye there, my pens an' papers,
For I maun up, an' to my scrapers—
Yet, min', my lass— ye maun return
This very night we cut the churn.

While some of the Staggers Point residents might have sounded like our stock leprechaun characters, and others like Southern hillbillies, if we listen hard, we can hear the roots of Southern backwoods dialect in this Ulster Scots, with its "ye"s and "whar"s and its dropped final consonants. "... pantin' wi' the heat" could have been spoken by an Irish mill worker or an Alabama farmer.

As mentioned, every Sunday, if at all possible, the entire household, slaves included, went to church. And during the summers they would attend "the protracted meetings,"[210] presumably tent revivals. One particular meeting in 1841 was remembered for fifty years. Harrison Owen wrote: "The new county will never be the same again. Some of the ruffians of Robertson County had all hell scared out of them. Never have I heard such preaching and I'm sure no one else has. ... I kept thinking of John the Baptist in the wilderness of Bible times, and I think the Methodist preachers were just

---

[210] Myrtle Murray, "Home Life on Ranches in Southwest Texas"

as impressive." Hundreds of settlers attended the meeting and there were more than twenty conversions.[211]

The preachers for these meetings were usually among the most upright of men the frontier could produce. But once, while a visiting "preacher" was going on and on, his partners were stealing horses outside. One of his horses was shot by men outside the prayer meeting trying to capture the thieves, and the horse reported straight to the meeting to find its owner. There, a slave rushed in and told the group that the preacher had men stealing the horses, but by then the preacher had skipped the scene. One knew better than to mess with a man's horse in those days. The men of the town chased the imposter and his accomplices to a thicket near Mumford where in a shootout they killed several of them including the "preacher."[212]

And no history of Staggers Point is complete without mention of the notorious Presbyterian minister Rev. Fullenwider, who preached in the settlement from the colonial period and whom area historian Jimmie Henry Rice remembered as a rugged individualist who was ready at all times to defend the Bible with his fists. Direct from Central Casting, it was said Fullenwider "preached the Gospel only on Sundays and used the other six days of the week to fight Indians, work in the fields, nurse the sick, marry the living, and bury the dead."

One story tells of a ruffian who promised to attend church if the minister could "whip him." Bad idea. Parson Fullenwider "gave him the licking of his life and then saved his soul."[213] Apparently, Reverend Fullenwider also liked the

---

[211] Baker, *A History of Robertson County*, p. 235.

[212] Baker, *A History of Robertson County*, p. 337. Another account says that the Staggers Point men chased the "preacher" all the way to the Mississippi River, where they summarily hanged him, but this chase of more than 350 miles seems highly unlikely. Perhaps he was hanged by the Little Brazos River, that runs passed Mumford, and over time "river" became "Mississippi River."

[213] Baker, *A History of Robertson County*, p. 237 & 337.

sound of his own voice, and would preach until one-thirty or two in the afternoon. Ever resourceful, Bettie would sneak bread from the communion plate to the children to keep them from crying in hunger as the reverend continued to save his congregants souls even as he imperiled their bodies.

In the same way that "everyone was a farmer" in some degree during this period and in this place, it is also true that virtually all religion on the frontier would be considered by today's observer to be fundamentalist. Protestants on the Texas frontier were generally Baptist, Methodist, or Presbyterian. While Methodism and Presbyterianism are today viewed as the very essence of moderation both in theology and in the tone of the Sunday morning sermon, with many Baptist congregations rapidly sliding to the center themselves, all of them would have been considered fire-and-brimstone conservatives by modern standards. We see this in the Henrys' conversation before leaving for Nacogdoches: "We believe that the Presbyterians are God's very own, don't we?" We see it in the fact that *Indian Depredations* memoirist John Wilbarger was none other than a Methodist minister, and in the account above the likening of Methodist ministers to John the Baptist, hardly a shrinking violet.

Though they strictly observed the Sabbath, and likely despaired for the souls of all those who did not narrowly hew to their interpretation of scripture, these bluestocking Presbyterians knew how to have fun too. Friends would ride horseback forty miles to attend a party or a dance at the Henrys'. They would bring in one Dr. Bill Rogers to fiddle for their square dances and enable the Virginia Reel. Noah Smithwick writes of that time and place:

> The floor was cleared for dancing. It mattered
> not that the floor was made of puncheons
> [split logs, flat-side up]. When young folks
> danced those days, they danced; they didn't
> glide around; they 'shuffled' and 'double

shuffled,' 'wired' and 'cut the pigeon's wing,' making the splinters fly. There were some of the boys, however, who were not provided with shoes, and moccasins were not adapted to that kind of dancing floor, and moreover they couldn't make noise enough, but their more fortunate brethren were not at all selfish or disposed to put on airs, so, when they had danced a turn, they generously exchanged footgear with the moccasined contingent and gave them the ring, and we just literally kicked every splinter off that floor before morning.[214]

On the Anglo frontier, the fiddle was the first instrument on the scene, it being both the most traditional and the most portable. But settlers would not long abide the lonely wail of its catgut strings, and they soon found ways of rounding out the sound. In this, white masters were all too happy to borrow from their black slaves, and soon, "patting Juba" was a standard "instrument" in any ensemble. Also known as "hambone," patting Juba is generally done while sitting and slapping the thighs (the hambone) and the torso to create a funky rhythm. The term "patting Juba" came from a black rhyme that was often used to get things rolling for the hambonist, sort of a black analog to "Patty Cake": "Juba this and Juba that and Juba killed a yellow cat." In the rhyme, Juba was a slave, and the "yellow cat," unbeknownst to many a smiling slave owner who clapped along, was the slave owner himself.

The adoption of hambone, of course, was followed by white appropriation of the African banjo, just as the slaves eventually appropriated the fiddle, the guitar, and other European imports. In the pursuit of entertainment settlers and slaves beat on gourds, boxes, sheets of tin, pots and pans, and anything else that presented itself. Judge R.M.

---

[214] Smithwick, *Evolution of a State*, p. 70.

Williamson, namesake of Williamson County north of Austin, would even remove his wooden leg and beat time with it on the floor.

Christmas was a blowout, marked by feasting and parties. For days, Bettie kept the women of the Henry household busy cooking cakes, pies, roasting turkeys, ham, and beef until the cupboards of the double-log home were bursting and ready for company.

And nothing got folks keyed up like a hunt. While Harvey Mitchell was living with the Seales and working as the tutor of their children, he was invited to go on a bear hunt on Christmas Day. Mr. Carter, his former employer, told him that some ladies were having a quilting, and that Miss Evetts and Miss Curd, "reigning belles of the Millican settlement," and several other young ladies would be there. Col. Mitchell eagerly accepted. He was a bachelor, and this was a rare chance to meet some of the fairer sex.

On the morning of Christmas Eve, Mitchell dressed in his Sunday best, a suit he had owned for two years but had hardly worn. He then rode thirty miles to the house of his previous employer, Mr. Carter, arriving at sundown. He found several men already there, all of them in buckskin from head to toe, armed with rifles and Bowie knives, and accompanied by a host of bear dogs. As advertised, several young ladies were also present. Mitchell reported that evening was delightful, and being the best dressed man there raised his hopes that the post-hunt party would be even better.

In the morning, after several more men and lovely ladies arrived, it was time for the hunt. The men and their dogs plunged into the creek bottom, and in less than a half hour the dogs picked up a fresh trail. The hunters raced through the cane breaks and thickets in pursuit of the howling dogs. Col. Mitchell tried to keep up, but being a novice and with his good suit catching on every briar, he soon found himself alone in the woods, with man and beast alike all out of sight and out of earshot.

Finally giving up the chase, he surveyed himself and to his horror found his face, hands, arms, and legs bleeding and his good suit in tatters. Worse, his dreams of Christmas dinner in the presence of beautiful women were exploded. Mitchell made his way back to the Carter home and hid behind a large oak. He waited there until he got the attention of Mr. Carter's ten-year-old son, whom he asked to fetch his horse. Without even saying goodbye, he mounted up and returned to the Seale home, where Susannah doctored his wounds. He swore that he would never again go on a bear hunt, and he never did.[215]

Second only to Christmas was the Fourth of July celebration, which usually took the form of a large picnic on the prairie near the Henry house. The common expression became, "We ate barbecue all day and danced all night." And Robert's friend Sam Houston was "frequently the orator of the day." After the speechifying was over, he would dance with the Henry girls and any others who were game.[216]

---

[215] Boyd, *Grandfather's Journal*, p. 51.
[216] Murray, "Home Life"

12.

Brave a Heap

FEAR OF INDIANS CONTINUED UNABATED. In one of his memoirs, Col. Harvey Mitchell tells of getting lost while deer hunting and of becoming panicked upon discovering fresh, well-defined moccasin tracks of seven "buck Indians":

> I had been taught from childhood that there was efficacy in prayer, and I dropped on my knees in the middle of that sandy old road, reverently holding on to my gun, and if ever a boy did pray honestly, earnestly and fervently, I was that boy. I prayed to God that if he would vouchsafe to me a safe return home from that expedition I would never go deer hunting again in this world ... I have never gone on a deer hunt since that day.[217]

This, mind you, was someone who had come to Texas partly for the opportunity to kill Indians and who had already served as a minuteman. (After this and the bear

---

[217] Brown, *Indian Wars and Pioneers of Texas.*

hunt fiasco, there wasn't much left that Col. Mitchell allowed himself to hunt; maybe he took up fishing.)

On that day that began this book, sometime after the Henrys' return home from the fort at Nacogdoches, the Comanches came calling, and foremost in Bettie's mind must have been the blood-soaked settlers trapped along the banks of the flooding Navasota. Once again, the men were away from the home — not that it would have mattered.

Seeing the Comanche approach, Bettie sent a child to the pasture to tell the men to hide the horses in the brush. The child jumbled the message and failed to convey the presence of the Comanches at all. Sensing no danger, the men turned the horses loose so that they might trot up to the house, a sight that normally would have pleased Bettie.

The Comanche band had closed to within a half mile. Realizing the mistake, Bettie ran to the lot, turned all the horses inside the corral, and drove them into the big stable, which had a one-pound lock with a key eight inches long.

The Comanches had surrounded the cabin now. She heard their steps behind her but went on, urging the horses to pass into the barn, pushing and slapping their haunches. As she pushed the last one in, adrenaline coursing through her tiny frame, she pushed the door to and locked it. Then, she turned to the one she presumed to be the chief, looked him coolly in the eye, and slipped the key into her pocket.

The Indians turned to the corn crib and pointed. Bettie, with her children now at her side, moved in front of the crib. She pointed to the crib and then to her children, indicating to them that the food was for her children, and that it was all that they had. A few minutes passed in silence, certainly enough time for the highlights of her life to flash before her mind's eye — her father's linen mill, her mother's reading assignments, meeting Robert, *The Jane* pitching its way across the North Atlantic, Charleston, Alabama,

Nacogdoches ...

Then the chief approached her slowly, patted her gently on the shoulder, and said, "Brave a heap... brave a heap."

With a signal to his band, the chief turned and rode away, followed by a trail of astonished warriors, leaving Bettie, no doubt more astonished than anyone, standing with her children before the corn crib's door.[218] The act of cool defiance had earned the chief's respect when perhaps nothing else would have, and fate blinked. We might surmise that if Bettie had "gone native" at that moment, her name from then on would have been "Brave a Heap," and it would have suited her. That night, the Comanches made eight miles, stole another family's cow and chickens, and drove away their horses.[219]

On another occasion, Bettie was sitting at her spinning wheel in the dog-trot breezeway of her double-log cabin. Indians had crept up softly onto her porch. By the time she noticed them, she and the children were surrounded and once again without male companionship. Again, Bettie could have screamed and run, with a predictable outcome. Instead, she quickly pointed to the fabric, and started pumping the spinning wheel to demonstrate what she was doing. The Indians became enchanted with the rhythm of her spinning wheel.[220] The leader commanded her to keep it going, and they began dancing on the thatched floor. Eventually tiring of this novelty, they simply moved on.[221] Her fast thinking and cool-headed approach had once again spared the family.

What effect the constant threat of attack had on the family's spirit is up for speculation, but likely it only fanned the flames of their will to settle this land, and, as any outside

---

[218] Murray, "Home Life," Pickrell, *Pioneer Women of Texas.*

[219] Betty Westbrook Trant Family Papers. Mrs. Trant suspects the author of this three-page typed document with hand-written edits to be Stell Hearne, a James Henry descendant. p. 1.

[220] Hazel Richardson, "The Irish of Staggers Point," p. 15.

[221] Betty Westbrook Trant Family Papers. p. 1.

threat will do, tied them more closely to each other. "Family tension, like problems of social order," writes Fehrenbach, "required a certain amount of affluence or leisure to sprout. The frontier family was functional, and maturity came earlier than it would probably ever arrive again. Work, hunger, danger, and terror could not be kept or disguised from young people. It was impossible for a boy or girl to create a false, or romantic, vision of the world. ... No Anglo-Celt child reached physical maturity without seeing babies born and people hurt, animals slaughtered and old folks die."[222]

Every day, it seemed, life on the frontier grew dangerous in novel and unpredictable ways. Every month seemed to bring a new and bizarre challenge, even as settlements grew larger and more numerous. In the late 1880s, Russians and the Turks started roaming the area, sometimes with a pet bear or two in tow, which they used to beg for food. On one such occasion Robert's nephew James Alexander Henry, known as "Whispering Jim," getting on in years and unable to help himself much, was sitting in his chair on the porch when one such gang stopped to force him to feed their bears. Mariah Anderson, a former slave[223] who still lived with James, happened to see and hear what was taking place. Just as they had started to turn the bear loose on Whispering Jim, Mariah fired a shot at their feet and barked, "The next one is for your heart!" They left quickly and she followed them over the hill, still packing heat and discharging another round every time they slowed. They never returned.[224]

Russians and Turks were not the only new arrivals to the rapidly diversifying area. When Hugh, Bettie's and Robert's eldest, was grown, he was awakened one night by a noise in the kitchen. Since houses had no screens yet and the windows were open, he slept with a loaded pistol under his pillow in case animals invaded. He clutched his pistol and

---

[222] Fehrenbach, *Lone Star*, p. 90

[223] This is speculation based on the original wording "a loyal soul."

[224] Henry, "The Henry Family," *Brazos County History*.

called out, "Who is there?" There was no answer, so again he said, "If you don't talk, I'll shoot." Again, no answer came, so he shot.

As the figure fell, he heard a voice say only, "Woman." Hugh lit a lantern. She was a gypsy dressed in men's clothing. Seeing she was gravely injured, Hugh sent his two oldest sons to fetch the nearest doctor, in Wheelock. The doctor arrived several hours later and reported that she was bleeding out. She had a sack on her containing jewels, money, and other trinkets. Apparently, she had climbed into the second story of the Cavitt home the night before. Hugh asked Dr. Cameron to tell the residents of Wheelock to come claim their belongings. When she had died, Hugh and his boys built a box, then buried the woman under an oak tree a short distance from the home. For years, Hugh's grandchildren and great-grandchildren were warned that if they didn't behave, "the gypsy would come alive and take them off."[225]

But failing health remained the biggest killer. Whispering Jim's youngest adult child, Jeannette, learned that he had dropsy, now known as edema, a condition in which water accumulates just below the skin. He did not have long to live. She and her husband, George, rode in a wagon enduring bitter cold to be at her father's bedside. They arrived too late; James was dead. Piling tragedy upon tragedy, Jeannette had contracted pneumonia from the ride and died within a few days, and so did her husband, George, leaving the children orphans.[226]

In February 1847, Eli's wife, Susannah, died. It was just more than a month after her forty-eighth birthday. She left little in the way of a historical legacy, with few references and no extant description of her to go on. But with ten

---

[225] Henry, "The Henry Family," *Brazos County History*.

[226] http://rememberus2.tripod.com/np91.htm#iin5798

children, her genetic legacy is great indeed. Eli buried her near a pond on his land between Big Cedar and Sand creeks and erected an obelisk tombstone that would one day bear his name as well.

The following year Eli married the widow Susan Copeland Bridgeman. One thing that becomes immediately clear in researching this age is how very common remarriage was. In this, Eli had quite a role model in his father, Thomas, who was widowed four times, and married five — including to not one but two "Rachel Baxter"s, the second being the niece of the first. (In genealogy, he is known as "Thomas of the Five Wives.") There's little question that Eli grieved as deeply as any at the loss of a love, the mother of his ten children, and a partner in an epic life, just as Susan grieved the loss of Mr. Bridgeman. But remarriage in that day was less a matter of falling head-over-heels in love with someone at a romantic prairie picnic or church social than it was a matter of survival. They simply needed one another's help and protection, and there wasn't a lot of time to waste. Romance was nice when it came, but for a haggard and distraught widow and widower, simple compatibility would suffice. Though some of Eli's children were grown, there were still four or five at home, and Susan brought her three children still at home to the new family as well. By all accounts the newlyweds passed the next decade in quiet contentment as life in Texas after annexation in 1845 settled into a brief Pax Americana. No children issued from this remarriage.

As we consider romance, photographs from the period prompt questions about how the genders related to one another and suggest that culturally, these families were far closer to the Puritans living two hundred years before them, than they are to us. Men parted their unruly hair haphazardly to the side and typically grew the longest beard they could. Women, whose faces never once in a lifetime made contact with makeup — nor would their bodies contact a razor — parted their hair down the middle, pulled it down and back tight, and covered it with a bonnet if they could, end of story. The word *primping* could not have been in their vocabulary. The public virtues on display in these portraits are dignity and modesty.

Beyond the period hair and dress, we are struck and haunted by the vacant expressionlessness of our subjects. There is nothing rarer in an antique photo than a smile, or even a knowing look. They stare out like extras in a zombie western. Compared to the relentless vivacity — real and contrived — of modern photos, they appear as waking corpses, Victorian ghosts. The uniformity of this expressionlessness naturally leads us to believe that our forebears simply never smiled. And indeed, it is not hard to believe that they had quite a bit less to smile about, as these pages testify. But there are other factors as well. When the Daguerrotype was introduced in 1839, one exposure took fifteen minutes. This was a huge improvement over earlier methods, which could take hours for a single exposure, let alone over the days that people had to sit for a formal portrait to be painted. But even if they could have held a smile — or any expression — for fifteen minutes, it wouldn't have occurred to them to smile because portraiture from time immemorial had been the art of remaining still. Moreover, photography was a luxury, something indulged in perhaps once or twice in a lifetime, and therefore the portrait sitting was a deadly serious and very formal occasion. (Perhaps our sober subjects were simply pondering the money they were spending at that moment.) What's more, standards of beauty change, and in the nineteenth century, a small, controlled mouth was considered more attractive than big mouth with full, bright lips, and *teeth*! Finally, smiling was associated with drunkenness. Life was hard, no doubt, but these other factors surely skew our perception of these characters to the serious and flatten their emotional legacy.

TEN YEARS AFTER SUSANNAH'S DEATH, IN 1857, Major Seale himself passed on and was laid next to Susannah in Seale's Neighborhood.[227] He was sixty-four, and he had indeed done some living. Born in North Carolina, married to Susannah in Georgia, his was a life of constant struggle that belies the placid eyes that gaze out from his only known photograph. He had fought — or at least fifed — against the British in 1812. He had ranged against Texas' Indians in 1835, fought the Mexicans at San Jacinto in 1836, fought the Creek Indians of Alabama and Florida after that, and returning to Texas, chased the Caddo of the Cross Timbers. Intermingled with these struggles, he fathered ten children, uprooted the family probably ten times, and served in local government whenever called on, all the while somehow putting food on the table and accumulating thousands of acres of land in east-central Texas.

The Seale boys would soldier on without the Major. Eli died intestate, and his estate was divvied up between his children the following year. Each of seven living children except young Thomas received more than a thousand acres of land. In addition, Eli's possessions at death included:

> One negro woman valued at $800
> One negro child five years old at $400
> One mare $80
> One waggon [sic] and three chains at $50
> Dun filly $125
> Pall[amino] mare $85
> Grey filly $55

---

[227] Eli and Susannah Seale are buried with a single, obelisk-shaped stone on a ranch east of Sand Road near Kurten. The stone is accompanied by a medallion marker placed by the Sons of the Republic of Texas. This, known as the "Seale-Gerke Cemetery" is a small unmarked fenced area completely overgrown with trees and underbrush and not visible from the road. Approximately ten other family members are buried in the plot, some with missing stones.

* * *

"I'll bet my money on the bob-tailed nag,
Somebody bet on the bay."

—*"Gwine to Run All Night" (De Camptown Races),*
Stephen Foster (1826-64)

BY THE 1860S STAGGERS POINT had developed several businesses, including a beef-pickling plant, and Clum sold four-year-old undressed "beeves" to the plant for pickling for which he was paid three dollars a head by the owner, Mr. Tullis. The pickled beef was then carried south to feed the railway workers who were bringing the Houston and Texas Central Railway north.[228]

And it had perhaps the first saddletree shop in Texas (a saddletree being the wooden — usually ash — frame of a saddle), owned by P.P. Jones.[229] Staggers Point had a functioning school, and, now free from Mexican law, it could have its own non-Catholic churches. Predictably, the Presbyterian "Old Irish Church" built out of logs by Robert was the first to go up.[230] The second church was called Red Top, and, as many churches did, served duty the rest of the week as a schoolhouse.[231]

But just as churches exerted their civilizing influence, gambling crept in just as early and just as surely, it seems, to undo it. Just as today, the race track would become both a source of economic activity and a magnet for the criminal element. As the first really organized Anglo-Texan sport,

---

[228] Smith, *American Descendants*, p. 272

[229] "Origins of Names of Robertson County," *The Hearne Democrat*, September 19, 1936, p.6.

[230] "Benchley, Texas" *Handbook of Texas,* This is sometimes referred to as the Old Ireland Church or Ole Ireland Church.

[231] *The Hearne Democrat*, September 4, 1936.

horse racing developed even before the revolution, from the 1820s, and by 1845 at least twenty-five Texas communities were breeding horses; most of them would have had tracks so that prospective buyers could test out the wares. Richer Texans were importing more expensive horses and forming jockey clubs. Soon a racing circuit formed along the Gulf Coast, including tracks at Houston, Galveston, and Velasco (modern Freeport).

A young Christopher Columbus "Clum' Seale, 1821-1893

*Elizabeth Henry Seale, 1833-1916, wife of Christopher
Columbus Seale and the oldest-lived of the Henry children*

Clum took an interest in horse breeding and after he
married Elizabeth Henry, moved to Red Top and even raced
horses on his property. As primitive as conditions were,
Clum's and Elizabeth's ranch could not have been Shangri
La, but it was enough to make quite an impression on a
young neighbor, who in 1932, wrote this breathless
remembrance of the place circa 1850:

> After she [Robert's and Bettie's daughter
> Elizabeth] became grown and married the
> dashing young Texan, Columbus Seale, they
> came like two nesting birds to a beautiful
> grove of majestic oak trees on a high hill one
> mile to the east of the Robert Henry home,
> and there layed out and builded their future

169

home. Of that home a brief statement is here submitted to which the reader's mind is earnestly brought. I do not suppose anybody ever visited that home in all these 82 years that was not struck with awe and admiration at its wonderful beauty and its great size. One can see at a glance that no one but a master could have layed out and built that home the way it was built and at the time it was built. The beautiful residence, yard and yard fence, kitchen, smoke-house and servant's house, the spacious stock yard, horse lots, cow lots, branding and sorting pens, cribs, barns, stables, cow sheds and harness houses, swine pens, pens and pastures and many other features that could be mentioned. A master architect would stand and wonder how it could all be done as it was done — surely no one ever saw it that did not conclude at once that it was a perfect ranch and ranch home. To go there and look at it now in its present state of preservation, notwithstanding for the last number of years none of the family have lived on the place and its care has been left to tenants mostly, until recent years when Columbus Seale III has lived on the place, is yet worth a trip there. See those logs in those out houses in a perfect state of preservation, sound as a dollar and yet they were placed there 82 years ago.

When I was a mere youth I had the good fortune of visiting that ranch and had plenty of time to size up the whole situation and this is about the way I saw it: That home with its beautiful yard, long line of stable, barns and sheds, fine blooded stock of all kinds in those lots, stables and adjoining pasture, several beautiful red faced girls, half grown, each riding and running their horses after the cows just like cow boys. It was a sight the like of which I had never heard of nor seen nor even dreamed of before. When I went back home twelve miles away to old Steep Hollow, and told my neighbor boy companions about what I saw they would not believe me. But from that time on I saw the world in a different light — it was a bigger and better place in which to live than I had ever seen before.

When you drive out on Highway 6 take time to go by and see this wonderful place as it is today and then imagine what it was about the time I saw it in the long ago, and your decision will be: 'He told us the truth.' For great sagacity, keen insight and forethought, and for unlimited energy and a masterful capacity for doing things in a big way and for making a success of everything he touched, C.C. Seale the elder had not an equal among all the men I have ever known. But when we are reminded that he had a daughter, a name sake of Bettie Henry, for his life's companion, who stood by him every inch of the way, no wonder that success came to them from everywhere.[232]

All of the other Seale children stood in the shadow of Clum. Some did better than others, but Clum was the alpha-male, and none competed with his pre-eminence in northern Brazos County. Nothing illustrates this as clearly as his tombstone, an impressive six-foot obelisk of polished gray marble and fine workmanship, except for the typo that marks his final resting place with "Columbus C. Seale." Fifteen feet away, little brother Brad rests beneath a plain upright stone, crooked and weather worn.

---

[232] A.W. Buchanan, *The Bryan Daily Eagle,* Bryan, Texas, October 4, 1932.

Bradford followed in his footsteps, not only by marrying a Henry girl, the youngest, Mary, but by becoming a horse breeder too. One of only two known photos of Brad shows him holding a prized horse named "Eland" in profile, Brad's legs bowed from a lifetime of riding. The Seale boys took their horses as far as Galveston to race.

Bradford Thomas Seale, bowlegged from a lifetime of riding, and his horse "Eland"

Bradford Thomas Seale, 1832-1898. We are told his hair was red.

Conjoined receipts for taxes paid on livestock held during 1863 by C.C. Seale ($186) and B.T. Seale ($37), filled out and signed in the beautiful hand of tax assessor-collector and "father of Brazos County" Harvey Mitchell, June 15, 1864.

Quarter horses were really the only race horses in Texas until after the Civil War, and the first quarter horse race in Texas was run over the Houston Course in 1840. We're given a glimpse of early Texas horse racing by Francis C. Sheridan, a Brit who had been sent by "Her Britannic Majesty" to scout the possibilities for British investors in the Republic. In his diary, he wrote of the Galveston track, to which Bird, also known as "Uncle Brad,"[233] and Clum would later take their horses:

---

[233] *Bryan Daily Eagle*, Obituary, December 6, 1898, p. 3.

> About a mile to the right of the burying
> ground is the race course, and considering
> that the horses must put up with Sand
> instead of Turf, a very good race course it is.
> Being a circle of about a mile & a half
> perfectly flat & railed all around. ... Of course
> the most animated conversation took place as
> to the relative merits of English and American
> Horses and the knowing ones of Galveston
> were loud in their expressions of hope that
> England would accept a challenge to run a
> horse against the famous American horse
> "Boston." 4 miles & stakes unlimited. I joined
> in the hope, for great as the advance as to
> breeding may be among the Yankee horses,
> they are still a long way behind us, & in my
> humble opinion, ever will be.[234]

Currency was scarce in the Republic of Texas, and so the
barter system was just as alive and well at the racetrack as
it was at the general store. *The Galvestonian* described a
mule race in 1840, a sweepstakes for a pair of "splendid
Silver Pitchers of the value of $200 in specie; mile heats, best
3 in 5, Gentlemen to ride their own mules." [235]

In those days, horse races started with a tap of the drum,[236]
possibly because attendees were saving the gunpowder for
each other. Racing, especially in the days of the republic, was
lively, when not deadly. Again, Mr. Sheridan:

> The most uncivilised place in Texas is I
> believe Houston the former Capital — I heard
> and read more outrage & blackguardism in
> that town during my stay on the coast

---

[234] Sheridan, *Galveston Island*, 49-50

[235] *The Galvestonian,* Galveston, April 4, 1840

[236] Malcolm McLean, *Fine Texas Horses: Their Pedigrees and Performance
1830-1845,* (Fort Worth: Texas Christian University Press, 1966). p. 3.

committed there, than throughout the whole of Texas. It is reckoned unsafe to attend the races there, or indeed to reside in the Town a week after them, so desperate is the Bowie-knifing & pistoling on these merry making occasions. At the last meeting of these *"gentlemen sportsmen"* one man was shot dead, a lady in the stand narrowly escaped with her life, & a general stabbing concluded the day's diversion — besides which the feelings of some gentlemen had been so hurt, that they were seen for days afterwards bobbing round the corners of the streets, to avoid the shot of or gain a favourable opportunity of shooting an acquaintance ...

As a fix, Sheridan recommended all law-abiding citizens should lynch the criminals. Then, he reasoned, the country would be safe for British investment.

It's hard to know just when the wildness peaked, but by 1850, William Dewees wrote from Columbus that "the Sons of Temperance have been organized in almost every village in this State. This has proved to us a great blessing!" He then goes on to report, too optimistically:

Where once resounded the coarse language and the brutal laugh of the inebriate, it is still and quiet. We feel that the bright day of temperance is dawning, and that soon myriads of worthless sots will be gathered under the banner of temperance, and become valuable and respected citizens. King Alcohol is the most powerful foe that remains for us to conquer, and we have reason to hope that his reign will from henceforth be of short duration.[237]

After the Civil War, when Bird and Clum probably did most of their horse breeding, thoroughbreds gradually supplanted the old quarter-milers as wealthier Texans imported and raised them. However, increasing state taxes on thoroughbreds were making them cost-prohibitive. Many tracks closed, and many Texans returned to the popular frontier-style match races. These short, two-horse races, similar to charro races, could be held anywhere there was a level clearing and soon became the norm.[238] In modern parlance, it was as if Formula One racing were eschewed for stock cars and illegal drag races.

* * *

Though it's not pleasant to consider Texas history in such paint-by-numbers terms, the two decades between 1825 and 1845 could be summed up thus: Brown people were being attacked by red people, so they invited white people to come live between them and the red people to absorb the arrows. White people came and brought black people, and the red attacked white and black. But the white turned out to be worse for the brown people than were the red. Once the white bested the brown in battle, the brown incited the red and the black to fight the white. The red did, and sometimes the black.

These are broad-brush strokes, and there are exceptions to every one of these statements: Juan Seguin and Juan Navarro fought for Texas. In the mode of "my enemy's enemy is my friend," Indians were only too happy to help Anglos hunt down and kill their own hereditary enemies in

---

237 Dewees, *Letters from an Early Settler of Texas*, p. 307.

238 Mary Lou LeCompte, "SPORTS," *Handbook of Texas Online* (http://www.tshaonline.org/handbook/online/articles/xzs01), accessed September 20, 2013. Published by the Texas State Historical Association.

neighboring tribes. Blacks fought for Texas and for Mexico. But most of the conflicts broke along color lines.

Soon enough, though, whites would be fighting each other in the deadliest conflict of them all.

3.
Dixie, and the Quickstep

Oh, yes, I am a Southern girl,
  And glory in the name,
And boast it with far greater pride
  Than glittering wealth and fame.
We envy not the Northern girl
  Her robes of beauty rare,
Though diamonds grace her snowy neck
  And pearls bedeck her hair.

CHORUS:
Hurrah! Hurrah!
  For the sunny South so dear;
Three cheers for the homespun dress
  The Southern ladies wear!

The homespun dress is plain, I know,
  My hat's palmetto, too;
But then it shows what Southern girls
  For Southern rights will do.
We send the bravest of our land
  To battle with the foe,
And we will lend a helping hand—
  We love the South, you know.

Now Northern goods are out of date;
  And since old Abe's blockade,
We Southern girls can be content
  With goods that's Southern made.
We send our sweethearts to the war;

But, dear girls, never mind—
Your soldier-love will ne'er forget
The girl he left behind.

The soldier is the lad for me—
A brave heart I adore;
And when the sunny South is free,
And when fighting is no more,
I'll choose me then a lover brave
From all that gallant band;
The soldier lad I love the best
Shall have my heart and hand.

The Southern land's a glorious land,
And has a glorious cause;
Then cheer, three cheers for Southern rights,
And for the Southern boys!
We scorn to wear a bit of silk,
A bit of Northern lace,
But make our homespun dresses up,
And wear them with a grace.

And now, young man, a word to you:
If you would win the fair,
Go to the field where honor calls,
And win your lady there.
Remember that our brightest smiles
Are for the true and brave,
And that our tears are all for those
Who fill a soldier's grave.—

—Carrie Belle Sinclair, "The Homespun Dress"
Popular Song of the Confederacy

IN THE LATE WINTER AND EARLY SPRING OF 1862, the *Monitor* and the *Merrimack* battled to a draw at Hampton Roads, Virginia. General Grant captured Fort Henry, which opened up Tennessee for the Union. Then he won a pyrrhic victory at
180

Shiloh, Tennessee, somehow losing more men in every category — death, injury, and capture — than the South in a process during which 3,482 souls met their maker in two days. And finally in the spring of 1862, conscription came to the Confederacy.

The first of the Seale boys to leave for the war was Thomas, who, at thirty-six, was between Bird and Clum in age. In 1862, Thomas wrote home to oldest brother, Clum, who at forty-one was not required to fight and saw fit not to.

Saturday the 26th, 1862

Mr. C.C. Seale,

Dear Brother, I received your letter from the hands of Sam Evetts, which give me much pleasure to hear from you. Sam got to us to day at Cotton Gin in Freestone County. We have camped within ½ mile of Cotton Gin for the Balance of the day. We as all well, except sore feet and sprained ankles. I have got a pain in my left hip that hurts me very much though I am standing the trip much better than I expected. I suppose you have heard that this Regiment has been ordered to Tenn. Since we have started, we are on our rowd now to Alexandria to take water to go to Tenn. We have march a hundred miles out of our way.

I am sorry to hear that you got crippled but I recon you will get over it soon. I have no news of any importance to write so will come to a close. Give my best respects to all the friends, and if Brad is still at home show him the letter. I would have written to him but did not know whether he would be at home or not. If you want to write direct your letter to

Alexandria on Red River. Nothing more at present. So farewell with my best respects,

Thos. Seale

Likely Bradford was already gone. Brad, then thirty, and older brother Jo rode to the county seat of Boonville and mustered into the Confederate Army.

Apparently forgetting that gunpowder had been part of warfare in the United States since earliest colonial times, the Confederacy proceeded to form a company called the Texas Lancers, as in fighting with lances, as in the Middle Ages. A weapons shortage had the South's best military minds seriously considering arming troops with lances and pikes. That spring, Methodist minister George Washington Carter received permission from Richmond to recruit a regiment of lancers. A set of resolutions provided for twenty regiments of "Southern pikemen," and in April an act was passed that two companies in each regiment be armed with pikes. "Strangely enough," one writer mused, "such foolishness met with the complete approval of the military leaders, and even General Lee wrote Col. Gorgas (chief of Confederate ordnance), saying, 'One thousand pikes should be sent to Gen. Jackson *if practicable.*'"[239] (Emphasis added.)

Highly publicized in Central Texas, the regiment was eventually advertised to be the only one of lancers in the South. Naturally the idea of being a lancer was quite popular among Texans facing the prospect of infantry service. Brad and Jo joined the Texas Lancers, also known as the Twenty-first Texas Cavalry[240],[241]. The horse culture from which they came might have saved their lives, as cavalrymen were not the bullet sponges that infantrymen were. Not that all war

[239] http://www.civilwarhome.com/weapons.htm

[240] http://www.nps.gov/civilwar/search-soldiers-detail.htm?soldier_id=671974ce-dc7a-df11-bf36-b8ac6f5d926a

[241] Ola Maye Henry, "The Fullertons of Alexander," *Brazos County History*, p. 223.

was not dangerous: at one point the horse of the Seale boys' relative George Fullerton was shot from underneath him and a Union bullet put a hole in George's hat, grazing his scalp. But there is dangerous and then there is perilous.

Alas, after all the hubbub, the lances never arrived, and so Bird and Jo rode with their pistols and rifles and with the rest of the company became regular, garden-variety cavalry. From Boonville they rode to Millican, then to Navasota, and then on to Shreveport, Louisiana, to join Rev. Carter's Brigade. This brigade was composed of three regiments under General John Bankhead Magruder. They were transferred to the front lines in Arkansas.

Soon after Carter's brigade arrived in the green mountains of Arkansas, the three colonels, who were having their own miniature Civil War, reached a boiling point and went their separate ways. In the divorce, the Twenty-fourth and Twenty-fifth were detached, and the men dismounted. Asking a horse man to get off his horse in wartime was a life-and-death proposition, as well as an injury to pride, so Carter quickly aligned his Twenty-first regiment with the cavalry brigade of Col. William Henry Parsons to prevent his men from losing their horses as the others had.

The Twenty-first served in the Trans-Mississippi Department as part of Parsons' Brigade for much of the war. Then it fell under the command of a general with a name second only to John Bankhead Magruder's: John Sappington Marmaduke. In April 1863, a year after the men had enlisted, Marmaduke invaded Missouri. On April 26, Marmaduke was pursuing the forces of Union general John McNeil when he ordered the Texas Brigade to raid Cape Girardeau on the Mississippi.

On the night of April 25, anticipating the Rebel attack, McNeil had evacuated the women and children via steamboat upriver. McNeil's forces totaled about four thousand. The first Confederate column arrived at Cape Girardeau early the next morning. With General

Marmaduke's full division then on the western edge of the city, the attack began around ten in the morning. Cavalry units from both sides made unsuccessful charges, the Federal troops being driven back by the South's superior cavalry forces and the Confederates being met with heavy fire from field artillery and gunfire from two of four surrounding forts. The fighting lasted four hours, and by about two in the afternoon, Marmaduke ordered his forces to withdraw. Some ten men died on each side, and nothing was truly gained by either belligerent. Though it was no Gettysburg, perhaps it was a fitting metaphor for the war itself, and was probably representative of much of the conflict that went relatively unnoticed from lacking the apocalyptic scale of the battles farther east.

Upon withdrawing to Arkansas, the Twenty-first remained in the southern part of the state and served as scouts and raiders in the region.

But once again, as in the Indian wars, the vagaries of violence and fate split the ranks of family and cast some to death while others lived on. Bird's older brother Thomas had been captured in the war and taken up the Mississippi on a crowded boat and then overland to Chicago and the infamous Camp Douglas, which had become a prison camp for thousands of Confederate soldiers in February 1862.

One would not expect a Civil War prison camp to be hygienic let alone pleasant. But by any comparison in history, Camp Douglas was an appalling hellscape. By the end of March, more than seven hundred prisoners had died.[242] In the spring of 1862, the camp held 8,962 Confederate prisoners.[243] The founder of the camp, which began as a

---

[242] Levy, 1999, p. 29, 40; Kelly, Dennis. *A History of Camp Douglas, Illinois, Union Prison, 1861–1865*, p. 47. National Park Service, Southeast Region, 1989.

[243] Heidler, p. 345

184

Union training ground, was no engineer and located the camp in a wet, low-lying area. It lacked sewers, and the prairie on which it was built could not absorb the waste from thousands of humans and horses. Making a very bad situation worse, the camp flooded with each rainfall. And winter brought a "sea of mud" when the ground was not frozen. When the camp opened, only one water hydrant worked. There was a severe shortage of latrines and medical facilities. One in eight prisoners died.

In the summer of 1862, Henry Whitney Bellows, president of the U.S. Sanitary Commission, which had been formed in response to these wartime epidemics, wrote to the commander, Lt. Col. William Hoffman, after visiting the camp:

> Sir, the amount of standing water, unpoliced grounds, of foul sinks, of unventilated and crowded barracks, of general disorder, of soil reeking miasmatic accretions, of rotten bones and emptying of camp kettles, is enough to drive a sanitarian to despair. I hope that no thought will be entertained of mending matters. The absolute abandonment of the spot seems to be the only judicious course. I do not believe that any amount of drainage would purge that soil loaded with accumulated filth or those barracks fetid with two stories of vermin and animal exhalations. Nothing but fire can cleanse them.[244]

It would be too late for Thomas and thousands of other unlucky soldiers — Confederates and Union soldiers forced to train at or guard the camp, as well as Union parolees.

A letter from a fellow Brazos County soldier, Erasmus Marr, to his brother Samuel (who would eventually become

---

[244] Levy, *A History of Camp Douglas*, p. 81-85

Jo's son-in-law by marrying Jo's daughter Jenny), paints a picture of how thousands of prisoners were taken north, and what conditions befell them:

April 13, 1863

Dear Brother

I now take the oppetunity of writing you a few lines to let you know that I am on the land of the living and in good health and on dixie soil. We had a rather hard time while the yankies had us. when taken we were crowded on board of boats like so many sheep without fire and ...in the coldest wether during the winter and kept there on board 19 days.... We were carried to Alom (Altom, Ill.) on the mississippi and then taken to Camp Douglass Chicago Ill. After we got their we done fine to what we had done upp to that time though our treatment told fearfully uppon us. Our company lost 12 men. Amongst them was Thomas Seale ...There was as much sickness in the rest of the regiment and also the balance of the prisners there. There was some 4 thousand. Some from evry state in the confederate states. We arrived at camp douglass on the 29th of Jan and left on the first day of April and come through Ill, Indiana, Ohio, Pennsylvania, and maryland to Baltimore and took water there by way of fortress monroe and from thence to city point on James river some 5 miles from where we were perolled and turned out from under yankie soil. I am heartily thankful to be out from them as I have just seen enough of them to heartily hate them and am more willing to fight them now more than ever. This my case seems to be true with all the prisoners that I have heard speak about it. Our officers are not yet exchanged or perolled yet but will soone be and we will be exchanged in a short time as exchanging is going on evry day and it is said that we will be sent back to Arkansas again soon.

Tell Brad Seale that Thomas died on the 19th of February with typhoid pneumonia. His sickness was of about ten days. He died in the hospital and had the best medical attention and nursing that could be given and that by his request of me I have in charge his effects which is 137 dollars. I would like to write you a long letter but as this is to best by some Misourians that is about to start from here to Little rock I have to close it to get done in time. There is a continued arival of our men that is from yankies prisons and a continued return of the same to there respective commands. There has been several thousand here for the last week, about 2 here now.

EE. Marr to S.B. Marr

I will write soon if I do not leave here but expect soon to be on the west side of the Mississippi.[245]

By the end of 1865, the official death toll at Camp Douglas had reached 4,454, far more than had been killed in most battles. But some have written that more than six thousand Confederate prisoners died from disease, starvation, and the bitterly cold winters. An 1880s memorial in Chicago's Oak Woods Cemetery states that six thousand Confederates are buried there in a mass grave.[246] Typhoid killed around 30,000 Confederate and 35,000 Union troops during the war. One out of every three people who contracted

---

[245] Boyd, *Grandfather's Journal*
[246] Levy, *A History of Camp Douglas*, p. 357

this disease died from it.[247]

The combination of new military technology and old-fashioned military tactics produced a scale of battle casualties both unprecedented and unrepeated in American history. As George Worthington Adams wrote, "The Civil War was fought in the very last years of the medical middle ages." Surgical patients were numbed with chloroform, ether, and whiskey. The technology of warfare, on the other hand, was light years ahead of the technology of medicine.[248]

So it is stunning to consider that more than *twice* as many men died in the Civil War from disease as from combat. And of those dead from diseases, as many as half died from intestinal diseases that easily would have been avoided if people had any idea that feces should be kept far away from drinking water: typhoid, diarrhea, and dysentery.[249] Thomas' downfall, typhoid, was the most deadly, causing a quarter of all deaths from disease. It was referred to as "camp fever" or simply "the fever." Non-existent sanitation and lack of clean drinking water were the culprits. Latrines, or "sinks," as they were known, were merely straight trenches, without poles or rails to hold on to, the edges filthy, the stench unimaginable. It was quick and easy for flies and other vermin to transport bacteria from the trench to what little food was on the menu. Indiscriminate urination contaminated drinking water as well, which in turn produced added diarrhea and dysentery to typhoid. "The best treatment available" to which Erasmus Marr's letter referred probably was a stimulant and purge including calomel, quinine, and carbonate of ammonia, turpentine, or brandy.[250]

Diarrhea and dysentery, known as "flux," made a complete run of the camps. Most soldiers also referred to it as

---

[247] http://www.civilwaracademy.com/civil-war-diseases.html

[248] http://www.civilwar.org/education/history/faq/

[249] http://www.civilwarhome.com/casualties.htm

[250] http://state-journal.com/spectrum/2011/09/24/disease-killed-more-soldiers-than-combat

"the quickstep," presumably for the mode of conveyance to the latrine it inspired in the sufferer. From 1861 to 1866, there were more than 1.7 million cases of diarrhea and dysentery resulting in 57,265 deaths, a figure that is no doubt low.[251] The Civil War was not merely America's bloodiest conflict, but also, in every sense of the word — and with apologies — its shittiest.

The youngest of the Seale boys, William, had also gone to war, and at just twenty, he died as well. We do not know how, but we know the odds are two-to-one it was from disease. His older and by then late brother Thomas had been his guardian since their father, Eli, had died in 1857. Thomas was unmarried and didn't own a house, so he boarded with sister Mary Ann and her husband, and since the schoolhouse was on their property, Thomas taught the children.

By the end of the war, William and Thomas abided together again, not in the cold soil of an Illinois mass grave, but perhaps on the sunny pasture near an eternal Big Cedar Creek, a Texas Elysian Field. Four Seale brothers had gone to war; two, the mounted ones, would return home.

And of the Henrys, Robert's nephew William, James' son, fought and survived all of the violence of the war only to die of dysentery on the way home to Staggers Point.[252]

The Twenty-first returned to Arkansas, where the lanceless Texas Lancers again scouted and raided for the cause of Southern sovereignty.[253] Bird and Jo saw a bit more action when Maj. Gen. Nathaniel Banks invaded Louisiana in 1864. Reminiscent of his father-in-law's near-miss at San

---

[251] http://state-journal.com/spectrum/2011/09/24/disease-killed-more-soldiers-than-combat

[252] http://rememberus2.tripod.com/np91.htm#iin5798

[253] Anne J. Bailey, "Twenty-first Texas Cavalry," *Handbook of Texas Online* (http://www.tshaonline.org/handbook/online/articles/qkt21)

Jacinto thirty years earlier, the regiment didn't arrive in time to take part in the fighting, but it did follow the Union army on its retreat down the Red River and fought numerous skirmishes with Union cavalry and infantry. Then Brad got sick, and went to convalesce at Waverly in East Texas.

Brazos County records also show that Clum was pressed into service as captain of a slave patrol beat. As these were compulsory and all white men were assigned to a "beat," it is difficult to know what to make of this. At one extreme, Clum might have fit the description given by former slave Lewis Clarke, who wrote of slave patrols that they were "the offscouring of all things; the refuse ... the tooth and tongues of serpents. They are ... the scum of stagnant pools, the exuvial, the worn-out skins of slave-holders. They are the meanest, and lowest, and worst of all creation," and that their officers were "like starved wharf rats" prowling the streets in search of victims.[254] At the other extreme, Clum might have simply been a name on a perfunctory list and made captain mostly because he was the most prominent land-owner in the district, and perhaps he did not ride the country roads of Brazos County checking travel passes of black people and apprehending and harassing those whose papers were not in order. But as he was a slave owner himself and captain of this patrol beat we might reasonably assume he was somewhere between these extremes, as his brothers would have been had they not been off at war. Without evidence to the contrary, he bears the stain of the society he prominently supported. (Jo also is listed in a patrol beat, presumably from before the time he and Brad

---

[254] *"Lewis Garrard Clarke, 1812-1897. Narrative of the Sufferings of Lewis Clarke, During a Captivity of more than Twenty-Five Years, Among the Algerines of Kentucky, One of the So Called Christian States of North America"* Documenting the American South, University of North Carolina at Chapel Hill.

mustered into the army.)

In April 1863, the same month Bird and Jo were following Marmaduke into Missouri, Bettie's and Robert's Hugh set out on a cattle drive from Staggers Point to Shreveport, Louisiana. His father, Robert, his brother-in-law Clum, and Harvey Mitchell, are listed among twenty men whose cattle he was driving. Hugh left a relatively detailed accounting of the drive in a little leather-bound notebook that remained in the family for more than a century. The journey was two hundred four miles, and they drove two hundred two head of cattle. The cattles' average weight was five hundred thirty-five pounds, and they brought an average price of nine and a half dollars each, bought by Confederate agents to feed the troops. The cattle were driven slowly enough so that, at fifteen miles a day, they could graze their way across the prairies and yet still gain weight as they went. The book records several purchases of feed along the way, probably for the horses that the cowboys were riding on and that were pulling the chuck wagon.

Midway through the book is a list of families in Staggers Point who were probably in need of help. Most of the men were away at war. One note lists a Mrs. Giving and lists her number of children, then a plus sign, which probably indicates there was a child on the way. In a parallel column is an amount of corn to be given to them.

The book indicates that they set out on April 1, 1863, but halted from April 24 to July 24. Marshall Brown, who inherited the book, speculates that perhaps they had found a grassy stretch along the Trinity where the cattle were allowed to fatten up.[255]

The final entry in the book, which was inherited by descendant Sam Henry, listed the articles Sam had bought in 1890:

One pair shoes - $1.75

---

[255] Marshall Brown, "The Cattle Drive," *American Descendants...*, p. 265.

Axe and handle - 1.10
Snuff - .20, Coffee - .50
One pair shoes - 1.25
Cotton, checks & thread - .20
Matches - .20
1 - Pair Shoes - 1.50

During the war, things remained lively, and dangerous, on the homefront at Staggers Point. Once Bettie discovered a burglar who had unlocked her money trunk and was transferring all of their Confederate notes into bags. She picked up the first gun in sight and held it on him until help came. The thief was taken into custody and never seen in the community again.

THE TWENTY-FIRST CAVALRY SAW ITS LAST action at the battle of Yellow Bayou on May 18, 1864. The spring of 1865 found the Twenty-first Texas near Hempstead, Texas, where forces were being organized to repel an invasion. But the officers and the rest of the men knew that the surrenders of Lee and Joseph Eggleston Johnston in the East spelled the end of the Confederacy. Though they were never defeated in battle, Company "I" could read the writing on the wall. They did not wait around for a formal surrender, and the soldiers returned to Brazos County organized as a company, just as they had left it three years before.

At Moseley's Ferry, where the Old San Antonio Road crossed the Brazos, the company disbanded with the strains of "Dixie" fading in their minds. The new veterans went their separate ways, returning to unfamiliar children, and wives as fertile as their farms were barren. Brad, Jo, and all other former combatants signed "amnesty oaths" to the United States, small forms the size of half a sheet. Jo's read:

I, Joseph Arnold Seale, do solemnly affirm in

the presence of Almighty God, that I will
henceforth faithfully support and defend the
Constitution of the United States and the
Union of the States thereunder, and that I
will in the like manner abide by and faithfully
support all laws and proclamations which
have been made during the existing rebellion
with reference to emancipation of slaves. So
help me God.[256]

Joseph Arnold Seale, 1822-1899

Clum had been too old to serve but had to take the oath

---

[256] Boyd, *Grandfather's Journal*, p. 338.

too since he was a public official, a county tax collector.[257]

When it came time for Robert's brother James to take the oath before the election of 1866, he said to his friend, "Well, Pierce, let's go to town and take that dom nasty oath." When they arrived, they were forced to march to a poll between two lines of bayonets, and Flop-eared Jim became irate. When asked how long he'd been in America, he bristled, "Forty years before you was born, dom your soul!" (One's own soul, as well as the souls of others, apparently was frequently "dommed.")

They then exchanged whatever Confederate money they had for U.S. currency, at about a thirty percent loss. Jo's records showed an exchange certificate indicating he should receive $920 for his $1,380 worth of Confederate money. It was never redeemed.[258]

The war had visited well-documented poverty on the South. Hogs and cattle had been sold or donated *en masse* to the Confederate troops for food.[259] Staples like coffee were scarce, and wishful pioneers made "coffee" from all manner of other things from corn meal to sweet potatoes to rye, which they parched to a dark brown to fool the eye if not the palate.[260] But they stubbornly wore their poverty as a badge of honor as embodied in the popular song of the day, "The Homespun Dress":

> Now Northern goods are out of date;
> And since old Abe's blockade,
> We Southern girls can be content
> With goods that's Southern made.

(Interestingly, some women spun yarn from the fur of live angora rabbits, who would patiently sit on the laps of the

---

[257] Boyd, *Grandfather's Journal*, p. 88.

[258] Boyd, *Grandfather's Journal*, p. 338

[259] Brazos County History, p. 87.

[260] Boyd, *Grandfather's Journal*. p. 85

spinners and consent to have their shedding fur ever-so-gently pulled away and spun right onto the spool.)[261]

For those who had lived, life went on. But no doubt they wondered what a thousand days of blood, sweat, tears, and diarrhea had bought them. In truth, the Civil War marked the end of the age of duels with the largest duel there had ever been — a duel in the collective. The struggle constituted the death throes of an age in which an overwrought sense of "honor" trumped everything else, including reason and ethics. This duel with their stronger and luckier Northern brothers had cost them nearly everything and gained them nothing except a criss-crossed flag around which subsequent generations would rally in vain and argue the meaning of.

---

[261] Boyd, *Grandfather's Journal*, p. 85

14.

'Times Is Hard, Money Is Scarce, and Darn Rascals Is Plenty'

The 1870s through the Letters of Augustus Franklin Seale

In this penultimate chapter, we surrender the pen to someone at the scene, well, almost at the scene.

Clum was the oldest of Eli's and Susannah's sons, and through the combination of a sort of informal primogeniture and his own ability had come to hold a disproportionate amount of wealth that came to "the boys" from Eli as well as influence in the community. One example is a document from 1876 that lists sixty-nine men Clum had been contracted to pay for work cutting a road from Bryan toward Hearne to the Robertson County line, presumably the original path for today's Texas Highway 6. Beside each name is the amount paid, and in another column, "axe," "shovel," or "pick." Brother Brad, then forty-four years old, was paid $2 for an unknown amount of work with a pick.

But with Clum's alpha-dog status among the Seale brothers came headaches aplenty. Augustus Franklin Seale, or "Frank," was the seventh of Eli's and Susannah's ten

197

children, born 1831 in Alabama. Fortunately for us, Frank moved out of the Claypan, first to Wise County, Texas, just west of Denton, and then across the Red River into Indian Territory. Moving away from the safety net of family proved a severe hardship for Frank but was a windfall for us because he had to write to get news from the area, settle accounts, and so on, and write he did. In an extraordinarily intact collection of eighteen letters from Frank to Clum between 1873 and 1879, we hear an authentic voice from that time — genteel if semi-literate, and relentless in his pursuit of favors and of his share of family property.

His handwriting varies widely — one guesses based on his pen, his surface, his health, and his state of mind. But at its best, his script is exquisite, something only seen today on wedding invitations, and a strange vehicle for conveying Frank's backwoods grammar and completely arbitrary spelling and punctuation, typical of the time.

Sadly we do not have Clum's responses — when he did respond. (From context we deduce those responses were far rarer than the needy Frank would have liked.) But even a one-sided conversation can be instructive. With their entertaining turns of speech, the seemingly endless litany of woes and pitiful pleas for help juxtaposed with hard-nosed haggling, these letters present a unique window on frontier life during the 1870s and the personality traits that life forged.

In reading the letters, a standard form emerges: 1. Acknowledgement of the previous letter ("Yours at hand...") or, more commonly, the complaint of "I have not heard from you" 2. A statement on the health of the family (Diagnoses are not sophisticated; people are generally either "up" or "down"), which is usually repeated or elaborated on before the closing 3. Quickly getting down to business: "I want you to give me money / sell me horses / tell me how much goats are bringing in Texas" and 4. Various closings from the obvious "Your brother" to the dramatic "Yours unto death," followed by the strangely formal signature for a letter to
198

one's own brother: "A.F. Seale."

The letters contain little to no punctuation, and capitalization of words was entirely random. For ease of reading, punctuation has been added, capitalization partially standardized, and paragraph breaks created. Spelling has not been changed.

Was Frank the Seales' prodigal son and black sheep of the family, or, as he would have us believe, simply an innocent victim of a string of bad luck? Whichever the case, he apparently was Christopher Columbus Seale's cross to bear for many years...

Wise Co. Texas

October the 21, 1873

Dear Brother,

I seat myself this evening to write you a few lines to let you know how we are. We are in tolerable health at this time. I have bin sick, but I am up at this time. My baby has bin sick, but she is up. The rest of the children is in good health at present. I hope when these few lines come to hand they will find you and famly all well. Give my respects to all of the connection.

Clum, I havent herd from there cince your leter which you riten June the first, which it was very disparing to me. That arangement has Broke me in my calculations. I would like to here from you and here what has bin dun with it. Clum, I don't know what to do. I have sold out my claim. I will have to give posesion in a few days. I don't know where I will go to yet. I think I will go to the Indi Nation. It is about 75 miles to the line of the nation. Clum, I cant bi land with nothing but the money. I can't bi land in the nation but I can live on it as long as I want it. I think I will go there if I don't find a place before I get there. I will start in a few days.

Clum, I want you and the other boys to manage that mater the best you can, for I can't come this fall. I want you or one of the other boys to act in my place, and I will be sadisfied what you do with it for I don't see any chance for me to live any longer. Times is hard, money is scarce, and darn rascals is plenty. A pore man has a bad chance. I must close. Don't write to me til you here from me again. I yet remains your affection Brother until Death.

A.F. Seale

Wise Co., Texas

24 of D., 1873

Dear Brother,

I seat my self this evening to write you a few lines to let you know where I am and what I am doing. I am a trying to make a crop. We are all in moderate health at present. I hope when those few lines came to hand they may find you and family all in good health and doing well. Give my love to Brad and famly.

Clum, I havent herd from any of you cince I left there. [Note that in the last letter he expressly told Clum NOT to write him until he heard from him again, since he claimed he was about to move.] I ritten to Jo sum time ago, but I haven't received any answer yet. I am aliveing in Wise Co. about 15 miles south west of Decator. I have but a little inprovement. I give one hundred dollars for it. I have got 16 acors. My corn has bin bit down twice, but it has come out. I am plowing it out this weak. It is very cold spring up here. I have sum notion of planting sum cotton this year. This inprovement is on a old survey. They tell me it hasent come in to market yet.

200

When it dus I would like to by sum of it.

I like this country better than any place I have found yet. It is very good land. It is very easy worked. It is a yellow sandy soil. It is good wheat land. It is a good hog country. Hogs looks well. I have got a start of hogs. Clum, I went up on the land in Hood Co. The man that boat [bought] it would not pay me any thing for mi work. I had to move sum where. I like Wise Co. better than I do Hood. We have better timber in Wise. I moved about fifty miles.

Clum, I ritten to Jo what I wanted but I havent got any answer from him. I want you to send me sum money if you can do so for I kneed it very bad. My children is nearly naked for close. If I don't get some money I don't know what to do for close for my children. I haven't got nary dollar on my place and I don't have any chance to make any one at present times as very hard here. I am in a tite at this time.

Clum, I thought Sam Marr would move up here. I thought if he did move he could bring me sum money, but I don't know what he is doing. I [want to know] what he ams on doing. I ritten to him sum time ago, but I haven't herd from him yet. I want you to write to me what old man Lafevor has done about my land. I must close. Direct your letters to Boyds Mill in Wise Co., Texas.

A.F. Seale

Fort Smith, Ark.

July 24th 1876 (Three years later)

C.C. Seale, Esq.

Bryan City, Texas

Dear Brother,

I am charged by the malice of an enemy of mine with stealing some hogs on Red River last winter. I am entirely innocent of the charge and will be very able to so show at the trial, which will not be until November. I am here in soil 250 miles away from my friends on Red River and the law requires that the securities for my offerance at court should come here to enter into the bond. I could give the security if they could go on the bond without coming up here. But I fear it will be hard to get them to come so far from home, so that I want you either to come and go on my bond or to send me 500$ which I can deposit in lieu of bail. I will have to do the one or the other or else remain in jail until November court.

My family and my business needs my attention, and besides jail is no place for me or for any innocent honest man. I will rely upon your making some arrangement to relieve me from this confinement. If you choose to send my the 500$ rather than come you can get a draft on St. Louis payable to my order and send it here in the care of Misters Duval and Cravens, my attys. Write to me at once.

Your brother,

A.F. Seale

Fort Smith

August 9, 1876

Dear Brother,

I will write to let you know that I have been put to a great deal of trouble by an enemy of mine and have been brought to here for trial for killing hogs wich this man claims as his. The charge I am entirely inicent of and will be able to prove so if I can get out to get my witnesses. They would not allow me to give bail before the commisioner at Denison, Texas. It will have to be given here. I have written to you before but
202

have not received no answer. I would like to have you to send me ($500.00) five hundred dollars so I can give bonds and go home to my family. I am now two hundred fifty miles from home. Please send it to me in care of Duval & Cravens, my lawyers.

Your brother,

A.F. Seale

Write as soon as you get this.

Fort Smith Arkansas

Chick it saw Nation

Pickins Co.

Aug the 21, 1876

Dear Brother,

I have seated my self this evening to write you a few lines to let you know how we are. My family are all in moderate health at present. Mr. Marrs famly are not well at present. They are at my house. I hope when those few lines come to hand they will find you and family all well and also Mr. Marison and famly well, for I am very much oblidge to Mr. Marison kindess to me. Clum, I never will forget my friends. I got home all wright. I was five days getting home. The first day went nine miles. I was trying to get Mr. Marrs out but I did not get him out. Col. Cravens done all he could. He had Mr. Marrs bond filled out, and I sined it before I left. I haven't heard any thing from him sence I left him. [End missing]

Indian Nation

Oct. 28, 1876

C.C. Seale

Yours of 21 & 23 at hand on yesterday. Contense noted. According to request will respond at once. I am at a loss to know what to do. I have not heard from my Attorney, Mr. Cravens, for some time. Have wrote him two letters, but no reply. Cannot imagine why I do not hear from him as I wished some infermation and told him to answer immediately. I have not been able to learn from Cravins whether or not my witnesses can be summoned by the Marshals or rather U.S. Court. I hardly know if I will be able to get more than one or two of my witnesses there or not. Two of them have run off from here. One died. One in such bad health he cannot go, and another has now got into trouble that he cannot go. So that only leaves me two or three to go with. There are one or two others but cannot get to see them.

As yet I have not been able under any circumstances to find out if my witnesses can be summoned. I am under the impression they can, but has not been done. And no prospect of it. The marshals are in here now, but nothing for me. They have summons for witnesses upon the other side. I think if Mr. Cravins could do no more that he could write me; at least answer my letters. I hardly think he is doing much in my favor. I learn that Foster, the witness for Archy [the plaintiff], is at Fort Smith and has been for some time. I have been trying to procure a warrant for Old Foster and his son also. I learn there is an old indictment for both at Dallas, and Sheriff has been after them before they came in the Nation. I have been after that but have not got it yet. I may, but fearful time too short. If I had that, I could get them both out of the way. I have the warrant for Archy. When he gets to Fort Smith he will be arrested. I hope I may get the others. I cannot find out where Archy is at, so may be possible he will not appear as he knows there is a warrant for him at Fort Smith.

I want you to be at Fort Smith by the 13 of November without fail. You must come. Your business is not so urgent but what you can come, because when I get to Fort Smith they will find me in jail again. And I do not want to get there again as I may wait two or three weeks before I get my trile. I am going to start here on the first day of November. I want you to send the check for the money on Fort Smith as I think it best, and send check in Registered letter to me there as the time is now so short that I cannot get it here. I cannot get but little money here. Cannot collect, and cotton now so low that I cannot sell at it. Have not sold any yet.

All the witnesses I take from here I must pay their way of money matters and getting ready to start and to take what witnesses I can get. But I want you to be sure and come as I may need help. The Archy party are doing all they can against me. If you come I want you to be sure and stop at Dallas and see the sheriff, if there are warrants for Author Foster and James Foster and get them. And have them in the Sheriff's name so he can arrest them before they appear against me.

If you cannot come, send check as directed for at least one hundred & fifty dollars. Also write to me at Fort Smith just as soon as you get this and give me all particulars. You wished to know if I am going by Rail. I am not, as I must go in the wagon so I can take all my witnesses' provisions. As I believe I have give you all the news, I shall close hoping to see you at Fort Smith. This leaves us all well.

I have been talking with some persons since I commenced my letter, and it seems to be the general impression that Archy will not appear, and the trile will be put off. So you must come if it is put off. I must have another bondsman, and I want you on my bond again if such should be the case.

Your brother,

A.F. Seale

Fort Smith, Arkansas

Jan. the 10, 1877

Clum,

Your leter came to hand on the 9 ninth of Jan. I was glad to here from you and to here that you all was well. Clum, I am not well at present but I am sum beter than I have bin. I have had a very bad cold. It setle on my lungs. I have had a very bad cough but I am beter at present. We have very cold weather up here. The snow has lay on the ground 19 days to day and it ant off yet.

Clum, I don't think it will be much longer be fore our case will be desied one way or tother. Mr. Marrs has gone home after more witness. He has bin gone 15 days to day. If he has good luck he will be back before many days, then our trile will com off. They are going to do all they can to send us up old Foster. He is going to do all he can against us. Old Archy is not here yet. Col. Walker told a friend of mine if Archy don't come they can't hurt Seale. I am going to see walker about it. Clum, if Marrs gets any witness we will have som show. If he dont, we will have a slim show to beet it.

Clum, this United States Cort is the god domist arangement I ever saw in my life. Clum, you have no idear unles you was here to here and see for your self. Clum, I am glad that you have ritten to me all about the contract. I am afrade I will have a dispute with him. He hasent done any thing yet but write out the list of witness for my self and Marrs. Col. Rodgers is doing very well. This court he is geting several caces. He tries to keep sober. He is a good lawyer if he will let whiskey alone.

Clum, if they send me to Little Rock I won't live my time out for I can't stand it in prison. If I should have to go there I want you and Mr. Marison to help me out for I know I can't stand it. Tell Brad write me. Give my respects to all inquireing friends. I must com to a close. Nothing more at present but remains yours,

A.F. Seale

Chickasaw Nation

Feb. the 5, A.D. 1877

Dear Brother,

I seat my self this morning to let you know where I am and how I am. I am in bad health at present. I got home on the third.

My trile come off the twenty second. I come out all wright. The Fosters swore several lies against us. There was no speaking on it. The jury was out about two minutes on it. It was the loist domn thing I ever saw. Clum, Col. Cravins stuck out for the hundred dollars. I told him I thought twenty five dollars would pay him big for what he had done. He sed I out to be thankful. I told him I was thankful the way the thing was decided, but I told him he was misstaken about the contract he had made with you. Then I shode him your leter. He red it. He sed you was misstaken. I sed to him he was misstaken but he contended for it, and I setled with him that away, but I told him he hadn't yearnt it. Col. Rodgers wasn't at the trile. He fell out of a stage, and the stage run over him. It broke his colar bone. It would a bin a good thing if it a had a broke his dam neck. He is a good lawyer if he would let whiskey alone.

Clum, I want you to setle with Lafevor, and I want you to calculate how we stand and write to me and let me know how much is coming to me for I need it very bad. This scrape has broke me. I want you to ster Lafever up for all. I have waited long enuf on him. Clum, I never got your last letter before I left Fort Smith. The last letter I received from you was dated Jan 2.

This leaves us all in moderate health except one of my boys is very sick. To day he has took cold. I must com to a close. Nothing more at present. But remains yours,

A.F. Seale

Feb. 20, 1877

Brother,

Being so much rain that it raised the river that I have not been able to send my letter to the office until now. And will pen you a few more lines, which is indeed sad news. Since I finished my letter, three of my children has been sick with the malaria fever. Monroe died with it. Was sick only nine days. Suffered terrible while he was sick, out of his mind most all the time. There is one down yet but on the mend. No more sickness in the family at present, and hope there will be no more.

I paid Col. Cravins one hundred and twenty dollars, which he contended for. My individual contract with him was $50.00. Yours was $100.00. If they would keep off the true bill. According to contract with you and him he is paid $70.00 more than is due him. As you have a recourse on him perhaps you may get back the $70.00, the best you can with him in the matter.

Hoping this may find you all well. Let me hear from you at once.

Your brother,

A.F. Seale

Chick a saw Nation

Dickins Co.

March the 22, 1877

Dear Brother,

I have seated my self this eveing to write you a few lines to let you know that we are at this time all of the famly are well except my self. I haven't bin well cence I got hom. I am very puny. My wife [and] boy has bin sick very ner two months. He is mending sloly at present. We have a hard time with sickness. I think he probly will get well. The doctor says it will take him about one year before he gets all write. His brain has bin infected.

Clum, it don't look like we will make any thing this year for the grashopers is as thick as I ever saw them. They are in my oats. They have just struck them. I am about redy to plant corn, but I don't think it is worth while to plant yet. I have bad luck. The hog colary [cholera] got away with my hogs... I haven't but one sow has got pigs.

Clum, you sed sumping in your letter about the land I sold to Lafever. I sold to him three hundred and thirty two achors at five dollars per achr. That was what Hanover made when he run it out. I want you to do the best you can with him and as soon as posable. I have two doctor bills to pay and want you to ster him up if he wont pay. I beleave I have give you all the knuse at present. Nothing more at present.

But remains yours truly un death,

A.F. Seale

Chickasaw Nation

May 14, 1877

Clum,

Yours at hand some time ago, but not having an opportunity to send to the office have delayed writing.

This leaves us all well at present but myself. I have not been very well since I returned from Fort Smith. You and Brad have all the papers fixed up for the lands. I let him have and send them to Gainesville where I will acknowledge them at once and return them to you. Do you think the Lafever land will bring at public auction what he owes me? How much do you hold his notes for now? What was the principal after making the deduction in the land? Also the amount of interest? Have you his note for both principal and interest? I am ready to attend to those papers just as soon as you and Brad send them.

Crops are only looking tolerably well for this country and time of year. We have had a great deal of wet cold weather, so much so that my oats, corn, and cotton is a little backward, but will have fine prospects for a good crop. Let me hear from you soon.

Your Brother

A.F. Seale

Dec. 5, 1877

Did you get that deed that I send you some time ago? I have not heard from you about it. Also what have you done in regard to the Lafever matter? Have you collected it or not or what do you think is got to be done? Let me hear about the deed and the Lafever matter at once. What is the very lowest figure you will take for fifty mares? This leaves us all well. Let me hear from you at once.

Your brother,

A.F. Seale

Feb. 27, 1878

Brother,

210

As it has been some time since I last heard from you. I thought I would drop you a few lines to let you know my situation. We are all well at present but had colds with the exception of myself. I have not been very well for some time past. I am sorry to inform you of the death of my wife [Tryphenia Parmer]. She died on the seventh of this month. She had the Pneumonia. She was sick only a few days not appearing very bad.

What have you and Lafever done about our matters, and what can you do with it now? I would like to have the matter settled in some way, particularly if it could be done without loosing any money. I am in need of the money and would like to have it if there are any chance in the world. Or I will trade the whole amount to you for the horse property if you will trade and your figures not to high on your horses.

I am at present left in rather a bad situation and I am getting along very well under circumstances. I have nothing more at present worth your attention but let me hear from you soon all about our matters.

Your Brother,

A.F. Seale

C.N. [Chickasaw Nation]

March 30, 1878

Clum,

Yours at hand some time ago. Have neglected to answer oweing to our horse trade. I hardly know what to say at present. The way that I am situated at present I do not know whether I want any more horses or not until after our next court. The loosing of my wife has thrown me all out of fix. But I will say this, that we can go on with our trade and see what can be done and then if the horses suits me when I see them, we will trade. If we wait much longer to trade or at least to make an effort, it will throw me most to late to drive and locate the stock.

You wanted to know what kind of mares I wanted. I can tell you exactly what I want. In the first place I want all mares from three to eight years, none older or younger. Then I want a good average animal, something that will breed fine from either a horse or jack. I do not want old stock nor Scaliwags. I want them to start a stock from. So you see about what I want. What will you charge me for a good 3 year old jack? I have a fine stallion 3 years old.

Now I want you to find the price of your mares such as I discribed and remember horses are low. Try and get your figures down where I can reach them.

I have wrote you several times to know what the principal of them notes are since you made that change and also the interest on them to date. Please give me the principal and interest to date, as I want to know if we should trade.

If there should be a trade made I would drive right away. When we can understand all about what is and can be done I will come down. Now recollect I want to see the stock before I close the trade. Give me full particulars about your stock and price and the amount of notes and interest. I also want to know what you will allow me for my Lafever debt. Now be liberal in this trade. I do not suppose you will ask me a shave on them notes.

This leaves us all well. I am done planting corn. It is very dry. Let me hear from you soon.

Yours,

A.F. Seale

C.N., Pickens Co.

May 14, 1878

Clum,

Yours of last month at hand some days. Contense noted. I am

fearful that you and I cannot trade. In the first place, I won't take no $500 for the Lafever place. I will put my Frank on it first if I am compelled to take it back. In the second place your stock is too high. I cannot pay such prices. You must recollect horses are very low at present everywhere and have been for a long time. Horses are higher here than in the States. And I cannot get any such prices for mine that I have to sell.

As I have not made a horse trade, perhaps you can fix me up with a better cattle or sheep trade. What are stock cattle and sheep worth in your country and are they any for sale? Can a man buy 200 or 300 goats and at what figure? I want good goats. One of my neighbors wants them.

Let me hear from you soon with prices of cattle & sheep. I expect to be down in a short time nothing preventing. This leaves my family all well at present. My little girl has been very low, but up and about again.

Your brother

A.F. Seale

C.N. Pickens Co.

Sept. 10, 1878

Clum,

Yours of last month at hand today. Will reply at once.

If you think the trade you speak of is the best you can do, let it go at that but do the best you can. What does the Lafever note amount to to date? You speak of securing rent on the place. Is it for the crop now growing, and for how much? Hold him still for it if you can as it will be that much more. If the party you sell too will pay cattle for the back payment and let me have them now it would suit me. I will take them at market prices.

I would have written you sooner but was gone north of here

213

in the Nation looking at the country. I have had terrible bad luck this summer. I lost all my crop by the hail in June. 40 acres corn, 12 acres cotton, 10 acres oats. So I have no crop but a few acres late corn. Everything on my place was distroyed, nothing left. Renters lost all their crops.

I also lost my stallion. He killed himself about a month ago. He was the finest horse in the country. I would not have taken $500 for him in cash. Those that was not hurt by the hail have fine crops. Corn is now offering at 15 to 20 cents. I have another 2 year old horse up which is going to make a fine stallion if I have luck with him.

This leaves us all well at present but have been a little on the sick list.

Your brother,

A.F. Seale

White Bead Hill, I.T. [Indian Territory]
Nov. 25, 1879

C.C. Seale

Bryant

Sir,

Yours at hand some days ago. It seems there are a misunderstanding in regard to our affairs, which I will explain. My part as I understand, I had and have yet no idea what amt you stated was due me and of the $500 paid you on first payment. Now Clum, please make out an accounting in full of what I owe you, itemizing it so I will understand it fully, and see exactly the balance due me out of the $500 paid, which I want you to send me a check for on St. Louis to White Bead Hill, I.T. in registered letter. I do not see why there is so much trouble about that place.

Now Clum, if Page should fail, when can you dispossess him and make another sale as will the land be sold at public sale?

Explain how the land can or must be disposed off should Page fail. But if any show in the world hold him too the sale so I can get my money out of the place as I am needing it and do not wish to be selling always and no money. You know such arrangements are no money to me. According to your last arrangements, I cannot expect any more untill January next, I suppose. Also, please state the balance due on the place, and how much in each payment.

Now Clum, I do not understand nothing about that lot arrangement. I know that Tom had a lot in Bryant, but had forgotten all about it. When was the lot sold? How long ago? And when was that money divided among us? And what did I get my interest in? Also what did it bring? I remember nothing of the sale nor of any division whatever. If you can show me when the sale was made & that I received my interest so that I understand the matter fully, it is all right. I cannot consent to sign any title untill I am fully convinced that I have got my amount equally with the balance of the boys.

As I have nothing more of interest I shall close. But I want you to explain to me all about our land and lot matter. Send me the amt due me to White Bead Hill in draft on St. Louis, in registered letter. We are all well.

Your brother,

A.F. Seale

White Bead Hill, Ind. Ter.,

Dec. 21 1879

C.C. Seale

Bryan

Dear Sir,

Yours of the 12th at hand some few days ago. It came up all right. But was under the impression the amount due me was something like $80.00 or at least you said so in one of your letters if am not badly mistaken. I want you also to give me a statement in full (itemized) of the amount I owed you. I want you to give me, and be sure and do it, all particulars partaining to the late trades. I want to know how I stand and what is due me, if anything which would let him out entirely.

Can't you make Page believe that you will sell him out, and if sold he will coope his money paid, which might hurry him up? But do the best as you know I want and must have money to buy cattle. I am rather at a loss to know how comes that my land fell short in that last survey. It looks to me, in my portion falling off that you boys got it in your lot. Or how is that? Has any of the other shares been surveyed? I know one thing, that Brad sold me more land than he had, some 22 ⅓ acres. Now I do not want to loose the 44 ⅔ acres you all most of got it, or where is the mistake? I want you to look it up. If you all got no more than me, all right. If more, I think you boys should make it good to me.

You never told me how much Page was to pay for that place or it seems to be a different matter to get the money on that land. I want you to do the best you can with Page. If there can be nothing more got out of him, I suppose you had better make another sale if you think best, with Harris, Reed arrange the trade and payments, so I can get my money and of it as an early date as possible, or as much can be got immediately and by the first or middle of March. I want to buy some cattle in the spring and want all the money I can get. You speak of Harris not having money enough to pay the $200 and pay Page his money back. I am of the opinion under circumstances that I ought to have my $200. Then if any more money on first payment let Page have it, as if the place was sold publicly Page would get more of his $500.

How much still remains behind unpaid. If any money on hand or collect any at any time remit as before, which will be satisfactory.

Let me hear from you at once what you have done and when

I can get more money, also when balance will be due. I will start to my old place on Red River on Tomorrow. My family is well with the exception of myself. I have been puny for some days.

Yours Respt.

A.F. Seale

15.

The Fluttering Sail Is Spread

As a reveler in the Fourth of July, and as a friend of Sam Houston, who staunchly opposed secession, perhaps Robert was not too broken up by his state's reunion with Old Glory. Or perhaps he assumed Texans would simply continue to change their national allegiance every ten to fifteen years forever, as they had ever since he had arrived in 1829.

Whatever the case, in October 1865, six months after Johnnie had come marching home, and the men of Robertson and Brazos counties were back to their gaunt wives and unfamiliar children and struggling corn and few remaining cattle, Robert Henry died. He was sixty-four, as Eli had been at death, an old man for that country in that time.[262] As he

---

[262] Robert Henry is buried at "John Kopecky Pasture," private property on the west side of Rye Loop Road, near but not in the Rye Henry Cemetery. The local (Bryan) chapter of the Daughters of the Republic of Texas is named for him, and his grave is accompanied by a historical marker reading: "One of victors in Battle of San Jacinto. Born in Ireland; came to America, 1820, and here to Robertson's Colony, 1832. A staunch Presbyterian, kept true to faith at risk of life. In 1836 War for Texas Independence, he served in 2nd Regt., Infantry, Texas Volunteers. Prominent in public life, he held Justice of Peace Court beneath shade trees. He married Elizabeth Downing, Londonderry, Ireland.; had 13 children. Their heirs include noted Texans." Note that while he was in Gillespie's 2nd Regiment and was at San Jacinto, the Myrtle Murray

219

drifted, we wonder if his mind wandered to the stone stables of Crebilly Castle and the clank of horses being shod in the chilly damp air off the Irish Sea's North Channel? Did he see Bettie's face, young and taut, rimmed in wedding lace? Did his ears ring with the crack of flint-lock rifles and thud of hooves as he chased Kickapoo and Comanche and Lipan Apache across as yet unnamed creeks and prairies? Did he hear the whine of mosquitoes at sundown and the distant murmur of Mexican soldiers in the San Jacinto delta? Could he still feel the first batch of cotton coming out of his brand-new horse gin, and taste Bettie's spareribs, and feel the callouses on his hands from the construction of his four hand-built homes?

Bettie would go on living and living. After being known to an earlier generation as Aunt Bettie, she became known all over the country as Grandma Henry, a diminutive widow and a matriarch extraordinaire.

In her widowed years, she lived with Mary and Brad and just across a pasture from Hugh Reed Henry, her "little groundhog," now grown into a pillar of the community and heir to his father's frenetic civic involvement. Hugh had inherited the northernmost quarter of his parents' land. This place was so improved it became a stopping place for the stage coaches when the stage line was established in 1866. There they changed out horses on the tri-weekly trips from Millican to Waco via Boonville, Wheelock, and Marlin.[263]

---

account says that Sam Houston personally sent him away to Dunn's Fort before the attack began.

[263] *The Hearne Democrat,* October 2, 1963.

We have no images of Robert Henry or of any of his brothers.
Perhaps the closest we can get to knowing what they might have
looked like is this painting of Robert and Bettie's son,
Hugh Reed Henry, 1822-1883.

When once Bettie walked across the pasture that separated Mary and Brad's home from Hugh's home, Hugh asked, "Mother, wasn't you afraid to those cattle?" to which she answered, "No, dear, I just took my apron and shooed them away."[264] (Hugh must have forgotten he was talking to the one who earlier in life had used her skirt to shoo away a panther.)

And within two years of Robert's passing, Bettie would witness the arrival of something far more transformative than even the war had been. She would see the arrival of the train.

_____

[264] Galloway et. al, *The Irish of Staggers Point*, p. 34.

Rail recast the whole civic landscape of America, as rail companies dictated municipal winners and losers, and we see that history writ small in this corner of east-central Texas. Staggers Point, Seale's Neighborhood, and even the county seat, Boonville, were all losers when the tracks of the Houston and Texas Central Railway were laid only a few miles west in a little town named for Stephen F. Austin's nephew, William Joel Bryan. Even Harvey Mitchell, Mr. Boonville, encouraged his neighbors move to Bryan because "that's where the future is." By 1866 Boonville was deserted except for an orphanage near the cemetery that eventually was abandoned.[265]

The locals knew that rail was coming. In 1858, Eli's son Thomas received a letter from P. Brumond of the Houston and Texas Central Railroad, saying, "I am in want of laborers and will pay you 25 doll. per month for negroes in cash notes..." He indicated that many neighbors were taking this deal. "I will take them. I need several hundred. The friend of this enterprise should lend me their forces for which [I] will pay them. I soon have the road within your reach."[266]

William Henry, Robert's nephew, gave some of the right of way for the railroad. The Houston and Texas Central Railroad became the HTC, which was then reconstituted in the vernacular as "Hell on Texas Cattle."

Robert's brother James actually dismantled his house and rebuilt it near the tracks so as to become a supplier of firewood for the trains, which at that time ran on wood. Soon, they were selling beef, eggs, and honey to the railroad crew. As the Irish railway workers would expire, the railroad foremen buried the "Irish Paddies" on the railroad property with a $5 gold piece in each casket and, doing nothing to alleviate the stereotype, a fifth of liquor.[267]

---

[265] Sheila Fields, "Remembering Boonville,"
http://heritagebrazos.blogspot.com/2011/08/remembering-boonville.html
[266] Seale Family Papers, 1841-1888, Letter from P. Brumond to Thomas Seale, Esq., Daughters of the Republic of Texas Library at the Alamo.

In 1867, the railroad passed through Bryan. By early 1868, the workers had laid the five miles of track heading north, and when the railroad bypassed Staggers Point two miles to the west, the old settlement, with its thirty-five years' worth of log cabin homes and split-rail corrals, emptied out. The sun set on Staggers Point and rose on a new town: Benchley.

The tiny town of Benchley still exists, though most Texans return a blank stare when it is mentioned. One must follow it with "five miles northwest of Bryan" to get a nod of recognition. The "Benchley" name adorns the birth and death certificates of many a Henry and Seale and though not geographically identical, Benchley is the descendant of Staggers Point and the heir of most of its DNA. As the story goes, the railroad needed a depot there, and the depot needed a name, and so a new town was born. All agree that it was named for Henry Benchley. Most local histories — even the authoritative *Handbook of Texas* — say that Benchley was named by the townspeople for their favorite railroad conductor. As of this writing, the *Handbook of Texas* states:

> The Houston and Texas Central Railway reached the site in 1868, and as the settlement developed into a town the citizens gave it the name Benchley, in honor of the first freight conductor, Henry Benchley. A telegraph station established at the depot was operated by a one-armed man named Squires, and a post office provided the community with mail service from 1882 into the 1950s...[268]

Another reference states, "Henry Benchley ... was conductor on the first train that pulled to a stop at a little

---

[267] Sam Rice, *American Descendants...*, "History of Benchley."
[268] James L. Hailey, "BENCHLEY, TX," *Handbook of Texas Online* (http://www.tshaonline.org/handbook/online/articles/hlb23), accessed October 04, 2013. Published by the Texas State Historical Association.

shack they had thrown together to be a place for the telegraph operator to stay and his wires were just tacked on a small poles and I imagine [he] went on to Hearne."[269]

While this would be quirky and quaint, and suggests a jolly conductor waving his blue-and-white cap to smiling townsfolk as he rolled through, the reality is a thousandfold more interesting: Henry Benchley, it seems, was not just any railroad operator. While he might have been that, he also was an operator on the *underground* railroad.

Henry Wetherby Benchley was born in Valley Forge, Pennsylvania, in 1822 and became a major player in American politics on the East Coast, indeed helping to found the Republican Party in the East. He was elected a state representative and state senator in Massachusetts and eventually became Massachusetts' lieutenant governor during 1856 and 1857. He might have risen to even greater political heights, but his outrage over slavery led the widower to leave his two sons with relatives and move to Texas. After arriving in Texas, he gave singing lessons in San Antonio and in Houston.[270] And there, he operated a station on the Underground Railroad helping slaves flee to the North. But he was found out, arrested, tried, and jailed in Houston. When the war ended, he was released but died in Houston in 1867 at age forty-five.[271] Benchley's grandson, Robert, became famous in the early twentieth century as a humorous writer and Hollywood actor. His great-grandson, Nathaniel, was a writer, and his great-great-grandson, Peter, became the most famous Benchley of them all, penning the 1970s sensation *Jaws*. Most of our information on Henry comes from passing references in biographies of his grandson Robert.

---

[269] Jimmie Henry Rice, "Items of Interest from Benchley," *The Hearne Democrat*, Jan. 26, 1967, p. 9.

[270] Avery F. Bon Blon Jr., "Letter to the Editor," *Waco News-Tribune*, October 24, 1962, p. 9.

[271] http://www.evi.com/q/where_did_henry_wetherby_benchley_die

Henry Wetherby Benchley, lieutenant governor of Massachusetts,
and namesake of tiny Benchley, Texas, in 1855. Ten years later he
would be sitting in a Houston jail for participating in the
Underground Railroad. His great-great-grandson, Peter, became one
of the best-selling novelists of the 1970s with his shark thriller Jaws.

But here, the story diverges into two versions that cannot be fitted together. In one version, found in Robert Benchley's biography, Henry founded the town of Benchley himself; this version is also the source of the claim of Underground Railroad involvement and jailing.[272] But in all the other histories of the area, it was the locals who named the town

---

[272] Billy Altman, *Laughter's Gentle Soul: The Life of Robert Benchley*, (New York: W.W. Norton & Co., 1997) p. 20.

after him, either because he was the conductor of the first train or because he was their favorite conductor. However there is an obvious problem with this: Henry Benchley died February 24, 1867, and the railroad reached Benchley in 1868. If both of those dates are correct, he could have never reached Benchley by rail; however, if either of them is off by even a little, it is possible he would have reached the area within a few months of expiring back in Houston. There is one source that says it was named for him "sometime later," but it couldn't have been much later because we see the name in use by the 1870s.

Given the area's history and the prevailing attitudes, it seems highly unlikely that the locals would have named their town for a convicted criminal and slave sympathizer, *if they had known his background.* If we overlay these two versions of the story, the only realistic scenario goes like this: Henry, the former lieutenant governor of Massachusetts, moves to Texas, operates a safehouse for slaves, is caught, tried, and jailed. At the war's conclusion, he's released in Houston. (Here, it is odd that he chooses to stay in Texas, but perhaps his memory of New England winters is too fresh, and apparently he does stay since we know he dies in Houston in February 1867.) Now a free man, he needs a job, and secures one with the new-fangled railroad running in and out of Houston. He conducts the first train to go north of Bryan (perhaps not all the way to Benchley), and the locals name the depot and eventually the town after him, knowing nothing of his storied past. But he dies shortly thereafter back in Houston.

So the only two realistic possibilities are: 1. He founded the town and the locals conveniently edited the story to become "we named it after the railroad conductor." (If he founded the town, he would have owned land there; and there's no evidence he did.) This leaves: 2. The locals did name it for him but knew nothing of his past, in which case the whole thing takes on a humorous overlay of poetic justice — a new town surrounded by formerly slave-worked plantations named for a convicted slave sympathizer. Weighing all the options and studying the timing, the second seems more likely. But there is also something about the timing that suggests the naming was a memorial. He dies in 1867; the town is named for him in 1868. Is there more to this story? Did he in fact have a history in the area beyond simply rolling through on a train? Was there a core group who named the town for him and *did* know his past? And is Benchley their quiet monument to his civil disobedience and his sacrifice, *so* quiet it has been effectively lost to history?

The truest answer might be found in a 1962 letter to the editor of the *Waco News-Tribune*. In the letter, Avery Bon Blon Jr. writes that it was not the people of the area who named the place at all. "When he passed away in 1867, the Houston and Texas Central Railroad thought enough of him to place a tombstone at his grave in Houston, Texas. In 1869, the H&TC platted a town at a place called Staggers Point, this they named in honor of Henry Witherly [sic] Benchley."[273]

The primal point of Benchley was a ten-by-twelve-foot telegraph station, manned by a Mr. Squires.[274] The first store was a general merchandise that sold dry goods, groceries, and all kinds of whiskeys and wines. The area still struggled to find enough teachers for the children of all its prodigious families. One report said that there were as many as seventy students being taught by one teacher. The first postmaster was one Mr. Chatham, who did the job with his one arm and was known, of course, as One-Armed Chatham.

By the early twentieth century, the telegraph booth that had started it all had been converted into a phone booth and a local paper proclaimed it "was all that was left of Benchley proper."[275]

Benchley remains a small town divided between

---

[273] Avery F. Bon Blon Jr., *Waco News-Tribune*, October 24, 1962, p. 9.

[274] *The Hearne Democrat*, September 4, 1936.

[275] *The Hearne Democrat,* June 20, 1941.

sprawling ranches with homes scarcely visible from the road, and a concentration of mobile and manufactured homes down a single road dubbed Benchley Drive. But its residents have long been realists about its country status and embrace it with self-deprecating humor. A *Hearne Democrat* column in 1961 by Jimmie Henry Rice reported on the release of a biography of Henry Benchley's famous grandson Robert with the following choice write-up:

"Some Benchley, Texas citizens weren't particularly pleased when I read them the passage from a biography of the late Robert Benchley, the renowned *New Yorker* magazine humorist and film comedian. This biography was written by Robert Benchley's talented son, Nathaniel, who is now a member of the *New Yorker* magazine's stable of authors.

"In this particular passage in the book, Nathaniel Benchley was commenting on his great-grandfather, Henry Weatherby [sic] Benchley, who came to Texas shortly before the Civil War: 'A small town in Brown County, Texas, was named for him (Henry Benchley). The last time anybody counted it had a population of 70 people, 12 of whom wanted to leave town but couldn't think of anywhere else to go,'" Nathaniel Benchley wrote.

Rice continued, "The 'Mayor' of Benchley, Rancher Frank B. Seale, had a reply. 'If 12 left, Benchley would be almost deserted. I don't know anyone who wants to leave the town. I must also admit that I don't know of anyone who wants to move to Benchley. This Nathaniel Benchley fellow did a little 'moving' himself when he shoved our town about 150 miles to the northwest into Brown County. When last I heard Robertson County was still collecting our taxes."[276]

Concurrent with the arrival of rail, Bettie saw the slow but steady march of technology in daily life. Candlelight was replaced by kerosene lamps. Not until 1869, five years after

---

[276] Jimmie Henry Rice, *The Hearne Democrat,* September 22, 1961, p. 8.

Robert passed, did she finally buy a cook stove, but she didn't like it. Biscuits were better, she claimed, cooked in her "skillet-and-lid." Spareribs were roasted to perfection on a hook before the fireplace. And potatoes were still the best ever when baked in ashes.

SHE HAD ENDURED AN INCREDIBLY DIFFICULT LIFE, and nothing testifies to that like the hard statistics — the birth and death dates of her own children. In all, Bettie gave birth to thirteen children in seventeen years. Of those, five died in infancy: William, 1824; Samuel, 1825; Robert, 1826; Ann, 1835; and Alexander, 1837.

Of the eight who survived infancy, three died in their twenties: John, b. 1822; James, b. 1829; and Stafford, b. 1832. One of these, we do not know which, was shot to death by an Indian as he rode behind Hugh on a horse. Two died in their thirties: Katherine (Kitty), b. 1827; and Margaret (Peg), b. 1830.

As Bettie lay on her deathbed in 1882, just three of her thirteen children were still alive: Hugh, the first born, outlived her by only one year, dying in 1883 at a respectable sixty-two. In 1892, Mary, the last-born and a wonder of fertility, died at fifty-four, having single-handedly given Bettie fifteen grandchildren. And only one, Elizabeth, b. 1833, the baby in the Navasota crossing story and the wife of Clum Seale, bested her mother's eighty-four years, living to a remarkable eighty-six and dying in 1919. Having lived so long and into the twentieth century, she must have been the source for many of the stories that survived.

*Mary Henry Seale, 1838-1892, the thirteenth and youngest child of
Bettie and Robert Henry, wife of Bradford Seale,
and mother of fifteen children*

But although frequently punctuated by sorrow, Bettie's was also a life of epic joy — one lived out upon a huge, blank canvas and painted in with an ocean voyage, horseback riding over flowering prairies, cooking and feasting, quilting and worshipping and square dancing, healing the sick and helping many another mother usher into this world the joys of their own lives. Henry neighbor A.W. Buchanan wrote in 1932, "She was recognized as the most remarkable as well as unique character that ever lived in Brazos County. From her great storehouse of rare wisdom brought to her keen mind by the long years of everyday experience, she was known far and near as one of the most interesting persons anyone ever met."[277]

On Saturday, May 6, 1882, Bettie Henry died.[278] On her gravestone beneath her name and the diagonal flourish "Born in Ireland," an inscription rendered almost illegible from more than one hundred thirty years of weathering reads: "Though lost to sight, to memory dear." It was a popular epitaph of the time, and it is not clear which came first, the epitaph or other songs and poems that contain the line. But one such work purported to be by the Irish poet Thomas Moore (1779-1852) must have been more apropos to Bettie than to almost any other person who lay beneath that line:

Sweetheart, good-bye! The fluttering sail
Is spread to waft me far from thee;
And soon before the favoring gale
My ship shall bound across the sea.
Perchance, all desolate and forlorn,
These eyes shall miss thee many a year;
But unforgotten every charm—
Though lost to sight, to memory dear.

Sweetheart, good-bye! One last embrace!
Oh, cruel fate, two souls to sever!
Yet in this heart's most sacred place
Thou, thou alone, shall dwell forever.
And still shall recollection trace
In fancy's mirror, ever near,
Each smile, each tear, upon that face—
Though lost to sight, to memory dear.

---

[277] A.W. Buchanan, *The Bryan Daily Eagle*, October 4, 1932.

[278] Bettie Henry is buried at the Red Top Cemetery or "the Seale Cemetery" in northern Brazos County. It is on private property no longer in the possession of the family. It is on a large ranch located at the southeast corner of the intersection of Old San Antonio Road (Texas OSR) and Highway 6. Bradford Seale and Mary Henry Seale are also in this same small cemetery.

Bettie and Robert's descendants and Eli and Susannah's descendants now number well into the hundreds and are scattered across America. Beginning in 1935 annual Henry family reunions began to draw as many as 500 people from across the state and beyond.[279] But nearly two hundred years on, many dozen remain within fifty miles of where the Henrys' ox-drawn covered wagon finally creaked to a halt on the banks of the Little Brazos River.

Bettie Downing Henry, 1798-1882

* * *

---

[279] These began at the centennial of the birth of Bud Henry, son of Robert's brother William.

Clum died in 1893 at the age of 72. We can imagine that shortly thereafter, the other Seale boys finally had their brief day in the sun. A *Galveston Daily News* item in 1896 announced: "Bryan, Brazos Co. Texas — A grand barbecue and basket dinner will be given Friday, July 17, in B.T. Seale's pasture near Benchley. About 2000 people are expected to attend. Hon. R.L. Henry,[280] democratic candidate for congress, is announced to speak, and other speakers will be present. Between 1200 and 1400 pounds of meat have already been secured for the barbecue. A dancing pavilion and a tournament track will be provided for the occasion."[281]

Bradford, who had moved to Mexican Texas as a toddler in the back of Eli's and Susannah's ox wagon, very nearly saw the twentieth century, dying in 1898, six years a widower. The headline of his obituary in the *Bryan Daily Eagle* reads: "Death of an Old and Respected Citizen." He was sixty-five.

---

[280] No relation to the Henrys of Benchley.

[281] *Galveston Daily News*, Galveston, Texas, July 15, 1896. p. 5

Double Cousins: While most first cousins share half of their DNA, in the children of Columbus Seale and Elizabeth Henry and of Bradford Seale and Mary Henry we have a very large set of first cousins with identical DNA because they all share the same four grandparents. Pictured above are, from left, Robert Henry Seale, son of Columbus and Elizabeth, and Horace Bradford Seale, fourteenth child of Bradford and Mary and the author's great-grandfather.

A good story is worth preserving for its own sake. These two families' lives perfectly bracketed the sweet spot of Texas history: they lived under four of Texas' six flags. They lived at a time when people made up everything as they went along — their homes, the route from here to there, their careers, the schools they desired for their children, the governments they wanted to live under. They were present at the creation, at a time of dizzying freedom and the deep satisfaction that must have come from creating your life at an elemental level from the rawest materials, but also at a time of terrible violence, moral confusion, oppression that debased both master and slave, painful clashes between incompatible cultures, frequent sorrow, and backbreaking labor at a scale we cannot imagine, all within a single lifetime.

But, for this author, the story also is a meditation on the extreme unlikelihood of one's own particular identity, if not existence. The what-if's pile up like compounding interest: Had Bettie and Robert not themselves survived childhood, what with the famine caused by the Mount Tambora explosion, or the typhoid epidemic that followed in Ireland... had they not turned back to port when they did, but pressed ahead into that North Atlantic storm, ... had Robert not made it through those untold Indian fights ... had Robert been a week earlier to Goliad ... had Houston not sent Robert to Dunn's Fort on the eve of San Jacinto (granted, it was a lopsided Texian victory, but victory is always cold comfort to the widows, of which there were nine created in that marsh) ... had the panther jumped Bettie instead of the colt ... had cholera or malaria or meningitis taken either or both of them ... had Bettie waited just one single night for the Navasota to recede before crossing it on horseback ... had Robert gone with brother Hugh to fight Chief Jose Maria at Horn Hill ... had Bettie screamed at the sight of the Comanches surrounding her cabin instead of showing a calm that signaled "heap" bravery ... had she not made it through thirteen childbirths, so that her very last child might become my great-great-grandmother ... would I be the person I am, or would I be at all?

Afterword

WHEN I WAS THIRTEEN, I traveled with my parents from our home in McAllen in deep South Texas three hundred seventy miles to the city of Bryan in east-central Texas. There, in the parking lot of a Luby's cafeteria, we rendezvoused with a gray-haired gentleman who led us north out of the city on Highway 6. In ten minutes he pulled over, unlocked a ranch gate, and led us down a red dirt road. For what seemed like a mile we bumped along, stopping at least three times to open other gates and lock them behind us. (The man, Edsel, taught me, a suburban boy, that on a ranch, you always left the gate just like you found it: open/open, closed/closed, locked/locked.)

At last we parked and killed the engine. There, inside a waist-high black iron fence and under a stand of large oaks, was a tiny cemetery. My parents and I piled out of our tan Pontiac with large sheets of butcher paper and crayons and proceeded to make rubbings of the tombstones of my great-great-grandparents, Bradford Thomas Seale and Mary Henry Seale.

I knew nothing about them. Not how they had gotten there, and not a single detail about what their lives were like. They had been dead for close to one hundred years.

Anne Seale Burkhart, the wife of Edsel, our escort that Saturday morning, was the great-great-grandchild of the original landowners, one of the four patriarchal/matriarchal couples of the Henry clan of east-central Texas. Within a day or two of arriving back home in McAllen, we received an envelope containing a high school paper Anne had written in

1939 called "Pioneer Ancestors."

The five-page double-spaced theme (quite good for high school work despite the B grade it received) related a series of remarkable vignettes about how her ancestors — my ancestors — had come from Ireland to Texas. Within a year or two, my parents received in the mail a clipped column from the *Dallas Morning News* that included a few paragraphs relating the same story, the one of how Bettie Henry had ridden her swimming horses across the flooding Navasota River to save her children from being murdered by Comanches.

These stories were quite unlike anything else I had encountered in my still new foray into genealogy, and while I would forget most of the details over the coming years, the stories and images lodged.

Decades passed, and three things happened concurrently. 1.) I grew up. 2.) I had the good fortune to become a writer by profession, and 3.) the internet was born, facilitating research on a scale never dreamed of by earlier generations. In middle age, I started digging around again, this time online, to see if I could find any more corroborating stories about Robert and Bettie Henry, and to my surprise I began to find them, one after another. Now a book on Texas pioneer women devoting a chapter to Bettie. Now a paragraph in a local history book. I discovered a rich source in county histories. The Brazos County History published in 1986 proved to be especially rich. And a Robertson County history contained one sentence that pointed me to a wonderfully evocative and detailed article in a 1940 issue of *The Cattleman* magazine based on the memories of great-grandson Robert Henry Seale. Each new source contained some clue or other that pointed me to an additional source, and after a month of this, I had compiled enough material that I resolved that I should write the definitive account of these people. This collection of vignettes from disparate sources seemed to be pregnant with the possibility of a book. These people bore witness to the creation of Texas in both

238

the political and social sense. They lived under four of the six flags of Texas.

The research and writing became both a treasure hunt and a brain teaser: Source A would contain stories 1, 2, and 3. Source B would contain stories 1, 2, and 4. Source C would contain stories 2, 3, and 4(b), a version of 4 that didn't quite agree with the version in Source B. And so I began the historian's ancient task of compiling the stories, overlaying them onto each other, and choosing the most likely versions from among those that didn't quite agree.

Concurrently, I began doing contextual research. I knew that they had sailed from Ireland in 1821. Although I didn't know the ship, a bit of light research could tell me what kind of ship they probably sailed on and where they probably sailed from. If I didn't know exactly what they saw when their ox wagon came to a halt at what would become Staggers Point, a little sifting of accounts from neighbors could tell me. And so the story grew both by the continuous infusion of new accounts and by some educated conjecture. In short, what you are holding is a little essay on my family's history that got badly out of hand.

SO WHY DOES THIS PERIOD so fascinate? I think it is because their lives were so very different from ours and yet they are just close enough for us to have a real glimpse of them. They lived before electrification, and yet we have photos of them. Their world and way of life was exotic and alien to us and yet it was at the heart of our civic and social formation. It looks different to us in the same way a tadpole looks different from a frog.

In *Future Shock*, Alvin Toeffler made the observation that George Washington would have far more to talk about with Julius Caesar than he would have with us, and the same could be said for these "magnificent barbarians," as Walraven described Texian pioneer revolutionaries, with their huge beards and Bowie knives, riding their horses across vast distances in buckskin and homespun — the women mastering every facet of the homefront in their long cotton dresses, themselves dead shots with the flint-lock rifle. And still they are only a few generations in our rear-view mirror; that juxtaposition — that life on the cusp between antiquity and modernity — is somehow key to our fascination. Close enough to see, yet far away enough to look so very strange.

Applying cool-eyed journalism to family history can be a challenge, in two respects. While it is natural to feel pride in the accomplishments one's ancestors, and conversely to feel shame at their shortcomings, we should check both of these emotions, for we can take no credit for those accomplishments, nor should we bear the blame for their sins. They were them; we are us.

For me, it all started with a very basic human question: Why am I here? Specifically, why do I live in Texas at the start of the twenty-first century?

And the short answer is, Comanches. Comanches prevented the Spanish from settling Texas. Comanches are why the Mexicans invited Anglos to settle its northern territory. Comanches are what made the land free for the asking, and for my ancestors, that price was exactly right.

—A.S., December 2014

Glossary of Words and Phrases

bloodcheese - head cheese made with blood, resulting in a much darker color.

candy pulling - or a "candy pull" is a party in which taffy or molasses candy is made.

carding - to cleanse, disentangle, and align fibers by the use of cards in preparation for spinning. One side of each card has an array of nail-like protrusions to quickly comb out the cotton or wool.

carryall - a light covered carriage for four or more persons, from the French *cariole*

cavayard - a drove of horses or mules, sometimes wild.

clabber - sour, curdled milk, cottage cheese

colary - cholera

dog-trot/dog-run - a roofed passage between two parts of a structure; a breezeway between to rooms of a cabin

Grange - An association of farmers founded in the United States in 1867. One of the branch lodges of this association. Origin: a building for storing grain; a granary

hardtack - A hard biscuit or bread made with only flour and water. Also called sea biscuit, sea bread, ship biscuit.

homespun - cloth made from yarn spun at home

horse gin - an inclined treadmill powered by a walking horse that provided power.

methyglen - a kind of mead or honey wine.

pidlock - an herbal remedy from Ireland, possibly a corruption of "burdock," the common name for *Arctium*.

puncheon floor - a rough floor formed by the flat edges of split logs

quickstep, the - diarrhea

rattlesnake watermelon - A Southern heirloom variety with beautifully patterned "rattlesnake" markings

remuda - a large herd of horses that working horses can be daily picked from

ribbon cane - a subtropical type of sugar cane that was once widely grown in the American South. The juice was extracted with horse- or mule-powered crushers, boiled in a flat pan like maple syrup, and used as a sweetener.

scalawag - low-grade farm animal. Later became a derogatory name for Southern whites that supported Reconstruction or the Republican Party.

splunge - tool resembling a wooden hoe used for lake muddying

staggers - "strivers," in Ulster Scots dialect.

Bibliography

Print

American Descendants of James and Margot (O'Hara) Henry of County Antrim, Ireland. Smith et al., 1992.

Autobiography of Sam Houston, Ed., Donald Day and Harry Herbert Ullom, University of Oklahoma Press, 1954.

Black Texans: A History of African Americans in Texas, 1528–1995 (2nd ed.), by Alwyn Barr, Norman: University of Oklahoma Press, 1996.

The Book of Camping and Woodcraft, Horace Kephart, Field and Stream, London, 1906.

The Book of Texas, by H.Y. Benedict and John Lomax, Garden City, N.Y., Doubleday, Page and company, 1916.

Brazos County History: Rich Past - Bright Future, Honoring the Texas Sesquicentennial 1836-1986. Brazos County Heritage and History Council, Family History Foundation. Ed. Glenna Fourman Brundidge, 1986.

Bryan Daily Eagle, multiple articles

Empire of the Summer Moon, by S.C. Gwynn, (Scribner, 2011).

Evolution of a State, or Reflections on Early Texas, Noah Smithwick, 1901.

Fine Texas Horses: Their Pedigrees and Performance 1830-1845, by Malcolm McLean, (Fort Worth: Texas Christian University Press, 1966).

Finns Leinster Journal, Kilkenny, Ireland

Freeman's Journal, Dublin, Ireland.

Galveston Daily News, multiple articles.

The Galvestonian, 1840.

Generations of Captivity: A History of African American Slaves, by Ira Berlin.

"Getting in Touch with Texas Roots," by Ann Melvin, *Dallas Morning News,* 1986.

Grandfather's Journal, by Jim Boyd, 2004.

Hearne Democrat, Articles from 1930s-1970s

A History of Camp Douglas, Illinois, Union Prison, 1861-1865, by Dennis Kelly, Dennis, National Park Service, Southeast Region, 1989.

History of Milam County, Texas, p. 179, by Lelia M. Batte, The Naylor Co., 1956.

A History of Robertson County, Texas, by J.W. Baker, Sponsored by the Robertson County Historical Survey Committee (Waco: Texian Press, 1970).

"Home Life on Early Ranches of Southwest Texas," Myrtle Murray, *The Cattleman* Magazine, February 1940.

Indian Depredations in Texas, by J.W. Wilbarger, Hutchings Printing House, Austin, 1889.

Indian Wars & Pioneers of Texas, by John Henry Brown (Austin: L.E. Daniell, c.1886).

The Irish of Staggers Point (booklet) by Katherine Galloway, et al.

Kansas History, "Childhood Death: The Health Care of Children on the Kansas Frontier," by Charles King, (Kansas State Historical Society, 1991).

Language, Discourse and Power in African American Culture, by Marcyliena H. Morgan (Cambridge: Cambridge University Press, 2002).

Laughter's Gentle Soul: A Biography of Robert Benchley, by Billy Altman, Norton, New York, 1997.

Letters from an Early Settler of Texas, by W.B. Dewees, (Texian Press: Waco, 1968).

Lone Star, by T.R. Fehrenbach, 1968

Lynching to Belong, by Cynthia Skove Nevels

Papers concerning Robertson's Colony, Malcolm D. McLean, Ed., 18 volumes. Arlington: UT Arlington Press) 1993.

"Pioneer Ancestors" by Anne Seale Burkhart, (school research paper), May 20, 1939, Bryan, Texas. Compiled from family papers.

Pioneer Women in Texas by Annie Doom Pickrell, Jenkins Publishing Company, The Pemberton Press, Austin and New York, 1928, 1970, Chapter: "Elizabeth Downing Henry" "Data contributed by Mrs. H.B. Granberry, Austin, Texas."

Historical Recollections of Robertson County Texas, Richard Denny Parker, The Anson Jones Press, Salado, Texas, 1955.

The Robertsons, the Sutherlands, and the Making of Texas, Anne H. Sutherland, Texas A&M Press, 2006.

Savage Frontier: Rangers, Riflemen, and Indian Wars in Texas, Stephen L. Moore, University of North Texas Press, Denton, Texas. Vol. I, 2002; Vol. II, 2006; Vol. III, 2007.

Tales of Old Texas, J. Frank Dobie, The University of Texas Press, 1928.

Texas: Original Narratives of Texas History and Adventure, by Mary Austin Holley, (Lexington, Ky.: J. Clarke & Co., 1836).

Texas History For High Schools and Colleges, Eugene

Barker. (Dallas: The Southwest Press, 1929).

Tri-Weekly Telegraph, Robertson County.

Twixt the Brazos and the Navasot, by Johnnie Stribling, 1978.

Waco News-Tribune, 1962.

The Writings of Sam Houston, Ed. Amelia W. Williams and Eugene C. Barker (Austin: University of Texas Press, 1941).

Online Sources

www.civilwarhome.com

www.deltafarmpress.com, Capooth

"Ghost Towns of Robertson County," by Katherine Galloway, 1975, www.robertsoncounty.info

Handbook of Texas Online, www.tshaonline.org/handbook/online, Texas State Historical Society, numerous articles.

www.heritagebrazos.com

History of Ireland, www.WesleyJohnston.com

www.IrishTimes.com

www.LifeontheBrazos.com

www.nps.gov/civilwar

www.statejournal.com

About the Author

Avrel Seale has been a newspaper reporter and columnist, a magazine editor, and a speechwriter and is the author of eight books. He lives in Austin, Texas, with his wife, Kirstin, and their three sons. His blog, "The Trailhead," can be found at avrelseale.wordpress.com. He is the great-great-great-grandson of Robert and Bettie Henry and Eli and Susannah Seale.

Other Books Available by this Author ...

Nonfiction:

The Hull, the Sail, and the Rudder: A Search for the Boundaries of the Body, Mind, and Soul

Dude: A Generation X Memoir

The Tree: A Spiritual Proposition, and Other Essays

True Freedom and the Wisdom of Virtue

Fiction:

The Secret of Suranesh

The Grand Merengue